CHESS

Mike Basman

Illustrated by Tim Benton

Consultants: Malcolm Pein and Jimmy Adams
Executive editor and Editor of *Chess* magazine

Hodder
Children's
Books

a division of Hodder Headline

Text copyright 1999 © Mike Basman
Illustrations copyright 1999 © Tim Benton
This edition published by Hodder Children's Books 2000

Edited by Nicola Barber
Designed by Fiona Webb
Series designed by Fiona Webb

The right of Mike Basman and Tim Benton to be identified as the author and illustrator of the work has been asserted by them in accordance with the Copyright, Designs and Patents Act 1988.

10 9 8 7 6 5 4 3 2 1

A catalogue record for this book is available from the British Library.

ISBN: 0 340 791624

All rights reserved. No part of this publication may be reproduced, stored in a retrieval system, or transmitted, in any form or by any means, without the prior written permission of the publisher, nor be otherwise circulated in any form of binding or cover other than that in which it is published and without a similar condition being imposed on the subsequent purchaser.

The information in this book has been thoroughly researched and checked for accuracy, and safety advice is given where appropriate. Neither the author nor the publishers can accept any responsibility for any loss, injury or damage incurred as a result of using this book.

Printed by Clays Ltd, St Ives plc

Hodder Children's Books
a division of Hodder Headline Limited
338 Euston Road
London NW1 3BH

 # Meet the author

Mike Basman has rarely been out of the chess headlines since he won his first chess tournament (the London Championship) at the age of 13.

He captained the English student team in 1967 in the legendary match against the USSR which ended in a 3 –1 win for England. Six years later he became British Champion. Now he scandalises the chess world with his outrageous openings, such as the Killer Grob, while teaching chess in schools and running the world's largest chess tournament, the UK Chess Challenge (35,000 participants – and rising!).

He says: 'People think nothing happens on the chess board, but it's like a non-stop disaster movie – even better, because you're right in the middle of it!'

Introduction

Chess is one of the most exciting battle games of all time, and you can take part in it – whatever your age. Boys and girls of seven, eight, nine – and younger – are taking up the game in their thousands and amazing adults by their skill. They often win against grown-ups, and even masters are not safe any more!

British youngsters Ruth Sheldon and Nicholas Pert recently won the World Championships held in Spain, and their success has been topped by Luke McShane, who is running up grandmaster scores at the age of 13!

This book gives you all you need to start your career as the chess whizz-kid on the block.

Chess is hip, cool – and it's definitely not square!

How to use this book

Most of this book can be read without a chess set, because there are lots of chess diagrams. But for some of the later chapters (six onwards), it may be useful to set up a chess board and make the moves shown in the book on the board as well.

Contents

1	Who plays chess?	6
2	Join the chess set!	10
3	Know the code	28
4	Warming up	32
5	The tricky rules	40
6	Into action	52
7	Winning ways	62
8	Winning by force	81
9	Getting the edge	92
10	Winning by tactics	96

The chess scene	110
Glossary	116
Answers	120
Index	125

Who plays chess?

BEGINNINGS • EQUIPMENT • IMPROVING

Chess is played all over the world (although 'Go' is slightly more popular in China, and 'Shogi' in Japan). In the United Kingdom by far the greatest number of players are under 12! Boys play more than girls, but the balance is shifting as more girls take up the game. The world's youngest grandmaster is 13 years old. However, old fogies should not give up – the oldest successful grandmaster is 67!

Board talk

Grandmaster is the top rank in chess below World Champion. There are about 500 grandmasters in the world; below them come the International Masters (see page 112).

How did chess begin?

Chess began in the 7th century in India, but it may have been played before. No one knows exactly who invented the game, or how it started. The game changed in the 15th century when two pieces (the queen and the bishop) became extra powerful, which meant that a genteel, slow-moving game became as fast and violent as a World War II battlefield! Games got much shorter, from 100 moves each to fewer than 40, and lasted only half an hour instead of several hours.

A game of skill

Chess is the ultimate battle game, and it is all skill. In this battle you have no weapons against the adversary except your own mind, your knowledge, your fighting spirit and the swiftness of your calculations.

The aim of the game is to capture the enemy king. This is called 'checkmate'. It happens once the king is attacked and cannot escape. On the way to victory you may destroy the enemy army, but you have not actually won until you have checkmated.

Enemy pieces can be captured (your piece moves into the square occupied by an enemy piece, and that piece is taken off the board). But when you checkmate the king, you don't actually remove the monarch from the board. The fact that the king is about to be captured ends the game.

Of course a game can also be drawn – when neither side can give checkmate, or when the players and armies are so evenly matched that neither side can win.

Who plays chess?

The equipment

Chess sets come in all shapes and sizes. Some sets are tiny pocket sets. People sometimes get them out and play on buses and trains, or in a restaurant – or during lunch breaks in the playground at school!

The best sets are the Staunton pattern sets, in plastic or wood, and you can get these from the suppliers given at the back of the book (see page 114). A good plastic set might cost the same as one CD; a good wooden set and board might cost the same as three or four CDs.

Many schools have chess clubs – over 1000 schools play in the UK Chess Challenge every year. Sometimes teachers run these clubs, sometimes a group of boys or girls start playing among themselves – it's up to each chess club how it is organised.

How to improve

Millions of people can play chess, but only a few play really well. Make sure you improve by going about it in the right way:

1 Read books on chess. This is a great way to pick up new ideas. It doesn't matter if you don't understand everything – something will get through.

2 Play! Play anybody: family, friends, at school, abroad. Never avoid playing in case you lose – losing is the best way to improve. Keep moving up the ranks by playing stronger and stronger opponents, from school chess to local tournaments, from minor sections to major, major to intermediate, intermediate to premier, premier to open, open to national. National to international (and beyond?).

Read and play!

Join the chess set!

PIECES • MOVES
• CHECK AND CHECKMATE • CASTLING

What's in a chess set? A chessboard has 64 squares, checkered black and white. There are 32 pieces – 16 on each side – with different sizes, shapes and powers. One army is white, the other black. On the board, the rows of squares going sideways are called ranks. The rows of squares going vertically are called files (see page 29). The diagonals are also very important – queens and bishops use them, as, to a lesser extent, do the pawns and kings.

These are the different pieces:

The pawns

There are eight pawns and they are the footsoldiers of the chess board. They can only move *forwards*, never back.

Join the chess set!

The rooks

There are two rooks, sometimes called castles. They are solid, dependable pieces. They move *straight*, up and down and sideways.

The knights

There are two knights. They are the jumpers, the prancers, the jesters of the chess board. They move in an *L-shape*.

The bishops

There are two bishops. They are sly, slippery, elegant pieces. Their move is *diagonal*.

The queen

There is only one queen. She is the power piece. She combines the moves of the rook and bishop, moving either *straight* or *diagonal*.

The king

There is only one king. The king is the heart and soul of the game. He is majestic, moving in all directions, but only *one square at a time*.

Join the chess set!

The moves

The armies assemble on the battlefield. The forces are equally balanced at the start of the game, although white has the first move, which gives white a slight advantage.

Before you start your battle, you must first learn a little more about each of the pieces. You can see how the rooks are placed on the corners, with the knights and bishops next to them. In the centre is the royal family – the king and queen. Placed in front, to protect the more valuable pieces, are the eight pawns.

The armies are far apart at the beginning of the game, at each end of the board, but after a few moves the first pieces come into contact and the battle starts...

We'll start from the lowest, and go up to the highest.

The pawn

The pawn can only move forwards: never back and never sideways. A pawn is worth one point. What it lacks in strength it makes up in numbers. It has seven friends.

THIS IS WHAT I LOOK LIKE IN BOARD DIAGRAMS

Join the chess set!

Pawns can move either one or two squares forward on their first go, but after that only a square at a time.

The way a pawn captures is unusual: one square diagonally forward, to either side. The enemy piece is then removed from the board, and the pawn takes its place. Like this:

Enemy piece under fire

Pawn triumphant

Enemy piece dead

It doesn't matter how powerful an enemy piece is – the pawn can always capture it (if it gets close enough). (This does not include the king. No piece can ever take a king.)

13

Join the chess set!

A pawn that reaches the end of the board can convert into a piece of higher value: a queen, rook, knight or bishop. As the queen is the strongest piece, the pawn usually chooses this.

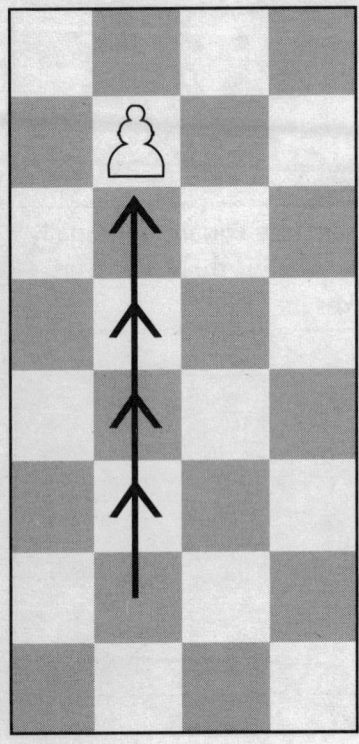

Pawn trips merrily towards end of board.

Pawn reaches end of board and turns into a queen.

You could have more than one queen on the board at the same time – up to nine!

This ♟♟♟♟♟♟♟♟ could be this ♛♛♛♛♛♛♛♛

+ the original ♛

Join the chess set!

Board talk

'Kibbitzers' is the name for spectators who hang around a game in progress.

The knight

The knight has a short range, but a dangerous movement.

THIS IS WHAT I LOOK LIKE IN BOARD DIAGRAMS

The knight jumps two squares straight in any direction, and then one to the side. It's an L-shaped move, which is especially powerful as the knight can jump over obstacles. A knight can move to up to eight different spaces around it:

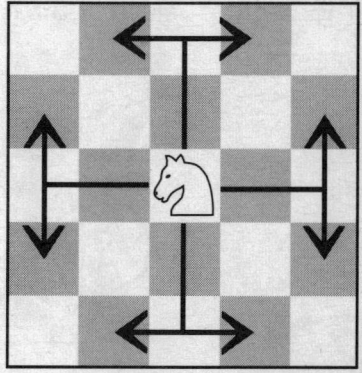

The knight captures the same way that it moves:

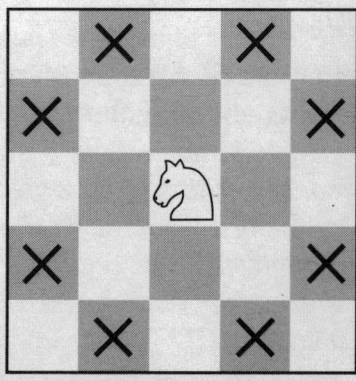

15

Join the chess set!

The knight fork is one of the most powerful weapons on the chess. This is when two or more enemy pieces are threatened by a knight attack. One of them can escape, but the other will be captured. Here a queen and rook are both threatened by the knight, and only one can escape.

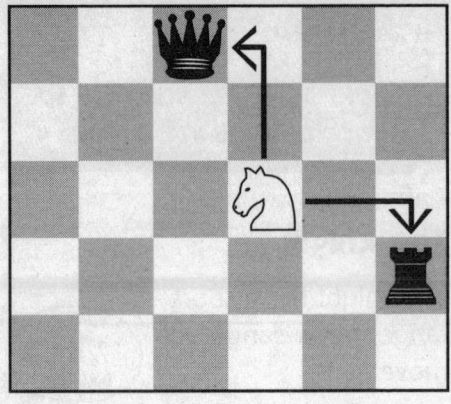

The knight is valued at three points.

Chess champs: Wilhelm Steinitz (World Champion 1886–94)

The founder of modern chess, Wilhelm Steinitz, was born in Austria and lived in Britain. A brilliant attacking player, he was also very obstinate. Once when a spectator made a stupid remark about a game, he compared him to a monkey examining a watch. Another time, he was asked by the rich Viennese banker, Gustave Epstein, to show more respect. He retorted: "In life, I am Steinitz and you are Epstein. On the chess board I am Epstein and you are Steinitz!"

Join the chess set!

The bishop

The knight and bishop are valued equally, at three points. But most experienced players put the bishop slightly above the knight.

The bishop is a long-range piece which can strike along the diagonals from one end of the board to the other. It captures in the same way that it moves and its maximum strike of squares is 13.

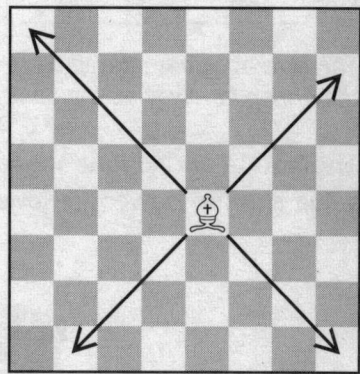

This long-range action should make the bishop almost twice as powerful as the knight (which can hit only eight squares). But the bishop has two serious drawbacks:

1 It can't jump over pieces.
2 It can only go on squares of one colour, so it is confined to half the squares of the board.

None the less, the bishop is a very agile piece, often weaving effortlessly between crowded pawns and pieces to strike a deadly blow to the enemy pieces and king.

Join the chess set!

The bishop, lurking in one corner of the board, carries off a rook.

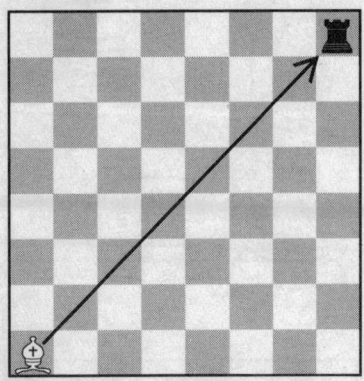 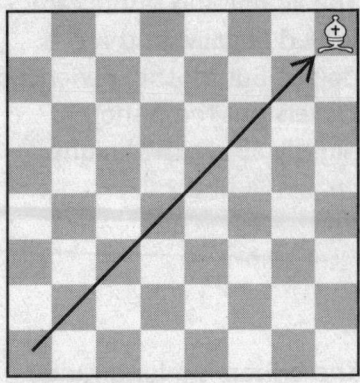

The black rook has strayed on to a vulnerable square, not noticing the bishop far away on the other side of the board.

The bishop and knight are called minor pieces, as their value and fire-power are lower than the queen and rook.

Board talk
A 'rabbit' is the name for a weak player!

18

Join the chess set!

The rook

The rook is valued at five points. It moves forwards, backwards and sideways as far as it likes. It cannot jump (unlike the knight) and this makes it a clumsy piece at the start of the game, as other pieces are constantly getting in the way.

THIS IS WHAT I LOOK LIKE IN BOARD DIAGRAMS

Unfortunately this tank-like piece cannot crush its own pawns underfoot, and so it must wait until a pawn has been captured, which then opens up an avenue for attack.

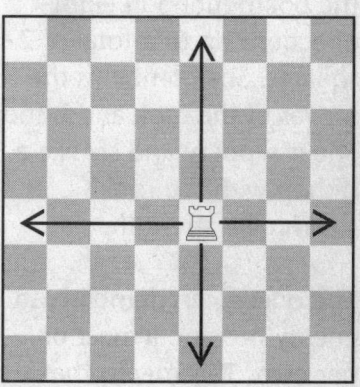

In the diagram below (left) the rook is shut in by its own pawns: it can't jump them. But there is an opening to the left, where a pawn has been captured. The rook moves to the opening (right) and can then attack vertically against the enemy black pawn.

Join the chess set!

Like the bishop, the rook also has a long range, but there is one important difference: the rook can reach all the squares of the chess board, which the bishop cannot.

The queen

The strongest piece of all is the queen. Splendid in her coronet, the queen dominates the board, firing in eight directions on to a total of 27 squares. She combines the moves of the rook and bishop. She is slippery and sly like a bishop with the rook's steamroller strength.

The queen can demolish an enemy position almost on her own. This means that you may have mixed feelings about her: on the one hand you can revel in her power, but on the other hand a single false step can mean the loss of your queen, and the possible ruin of your game.

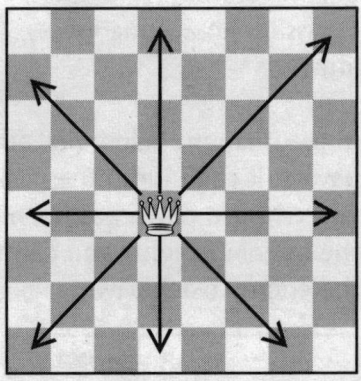

Few strong players bring their queen out early in the game, because she will be set upon by all the weaker enemy pieces. But when the way is clear, her power is devastating.

The queen is worth nine points.

The king

The king reminds us of the need for caution. Amid all the turmoil and hurly-burly of battle, the king stays in the rear. It is not for him to advance in front of his troops.

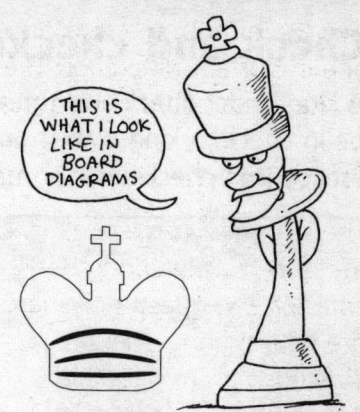

The king's move is rather slow: one square anywhere. So he resembles a short-range queen. Nonetheless, he manages to strike at a total of eight squares – quite a respectable number – though his range is even less than that of the knight.

A king may take pieces that are on the next square to him:

However, it is not his plodding movement that gives the king his special character, but his position as head of the army. The king cannot be treated like any ordinary piece or pawn. According to the rules of chess, the game ends if the king cannot avoid capture.

This special rule colours the whole game. If you lose any other piece – a pawn, a rook, a queen – the game can still go on, but lose the king and the game is over.

Join the chess set!

Check and checkmate

A king under attack and threatened with capture is said to be in check. A king who is under attack where there is no escape is in checkmate, or mated.

Check

Great care is taken to protect the king from danger, especially at the beginning of the game when so many pieces roam the board. A king in check must escape immediately.

Here we see a classic checkmate, delivered by a queen and bishop team. The queen comes close up to the king, and attacks not only the king but also the escape squares around him. Nor can the king capture the queen. Even though he can can move one square anywhere, if he

Checkmate

takes the queen he walks into the fire of the enemy bishop, who has been placed there to support the queen's assault.

Join the chess set!

Fortunately for the king, his life does not usually end abruptly in checkmate. Although there are many powerful pieces on the board, the pawns slow things down. They muffle the fire-power of the pieces, and can form a shield which protects against attack.

Chess champs: Emanuel Lasker (World Champion 1894–1921)

A great philosopher and friend of Albert Einstein, Emanuel Lasker would lure his opponent into unfathomable complications, where only a player with nerves of steel (usually Lasker) could emerge triumphant.

Join the chess set!

Castling – protect your king!

You can use the blanketing power of the pawns to set up a strong fortress for your king. Once in every game, if you have cleared the spaces between king and rook you can castle your king into safety. Here is how it is done:

The king moves TWO spaces towards the rook, and the rook jumps over him, and stands alongside.

See the bank of pawns now in front of the king? There would not be much point in castling without them.

Join the chess set!

You can castle on the other side too, with the other rook. This is called castling on the queen-side, and the rule is just the same: the king moves TWO squares towards the rook, and the rook jumps over and stands alongside. Like this:

Chess champs: Alexander Alekhine
World Champion 1927–46 (except 1935–7)

Alexander Alekhine was a classic champion and possibly the all-time greatest attacking player. He was totally obsessed with chess. Once he was a guest of honour at a theatre performance – but Alekhine never once took his eyes off his pocket chess set!

Join the chess set!

Quick reference

PAWN 1 point Moves forward one square, can go two on its first go. Captures diagonally. Can promote to queen, rook, knight or bishop if it gets to the end of the board.

KNIGHT 3 points Jumps two straight, one to the side.

BISHOP 3 points Moves diagonally. Restricted to squares of one colour. Long-range piece.

ROOK 5 points Up, down, sideways, as far as it likes. Long-range piece.

QUEEN 9 points Combines the moves of rook and bishop (straight and diagonal). Can hit 27 squares. The strongest piece.

KING Priceless Only moves one square anywhere, but needs to be protected against checkmate.

Join the chess set!

Board talk
Winning the exchange means winning a rook in exchange for a bishop or a knight.

Your first game

Now you will want to try out your moves on the chessboard. You may begin by playing against another beginner, but if you pick an experienced player instead, remember to be suitably humble!

- Set up the board as shown on page 12, and make sure that there is a white square in the right-hand corner, whether you are white or black.
- The white queen goes on a white square, and the black queen on a black square.
- The white player always moves first in chess, and then you take it in turns.

Who is going to start? This is usually decided by tossing a coin, or hiding a white pawn and a black pawn in different hands behind your back and getting your opponent to pick a hand.

Done that? Well, off you go!

Know the code

NOTATION • CODE CHECKLIST

When you have played a few games, you may have found a few things that puzzled you. Above all, you will want to be able to play better. The key to improving your game is learning to read chess moves. This is a valuable skill. It takes only a few minutes to do, and it will help you to follow the games explained here, and allow you to test yourself later in the book.

Each of the 64 squares on the chessboard has a name, based on a grid system. By joining up the numbers and letters we can give each square an individual name. This is called notation.

Know the code

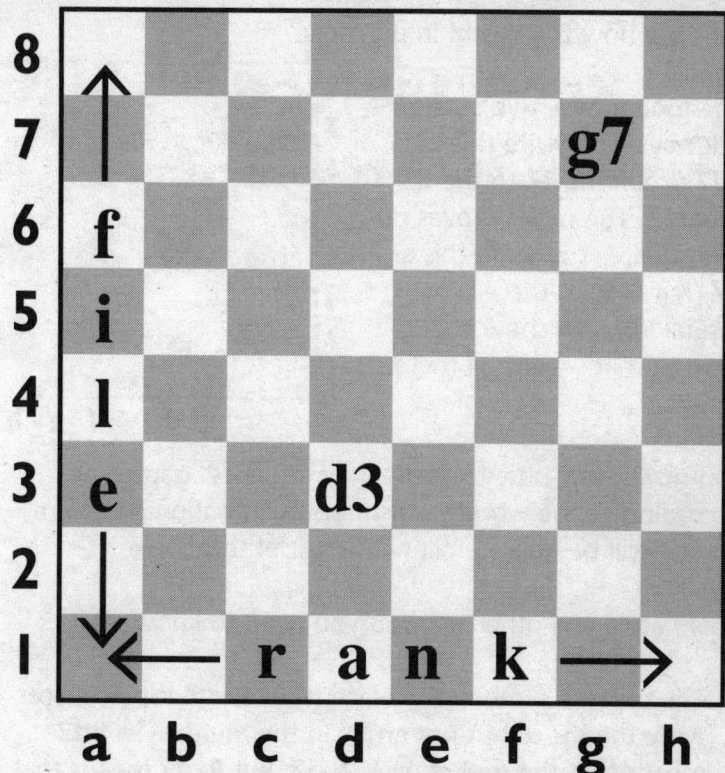

The diagram above names d3 and g7. Can you find f2? h8? b6? a2?

Just as each square has a name, so each piece has a letter to stand for its name. The letter for a rook is (guess what?) R!

Queen = Q
King = K
Rook = R
Bishop = B
Knight = N (because the king pulled rank and bagged the letter 'K' first.)

As for the pawns, there are so many of them that calling them 'P' wouldn't help, so the pawn doesn't have a letter.

Know the code

Let's see how this works in practice:

The rook moves two squares sideways. You write this as **Rd2** ('rook moves to the d2 square'). The pawn moves up one square. You write this as **d7** (remember, there is no capital letter to show a pawn). That's really all there is to it.

You now know how to read and write chess games, according to the world's most popular notational system. So you will be able to follow the rest of this book.

There are a few other symbols you need to know.

1. The capture symbol. If a piece takes another piece, you write the move but put an 'x' in the middle. So **Rd2** means that the rook moves to d2. But **Rxd2** means that the rook takes something on d2.

2. Check and checkmate. A king under threat is said to be in check. A king under attack from which there is no escape is said to be checkmated. The symbol for check is + ; for checkmate it is ++ . So **Rd2+** means: rook moves to d2 check. **Rd2++** means: rook moves to d2 and also checkmates the enemy king. (There are more details on check and checkmate on p32–4.)

3. Castling. Once in every game a king can castle. If he castles on his side (the 'short' side) you write **0-0**. If he castles on the queen-side (the 'long' side) you write **0-0-0**.

Know the code

Recording rap

Nought dash nought is castles short,
Three gongs is castles long.
One plus, you're in check,
Two pluses and you hit the deck.
Want to capture – put an 'x'
Guaranteed to get respect.
Place your queens remember where?
Same colour, same square!
One more thing before you move –
White pieces, rows one and two.
Black pieces on seven and eight.
Let's get started I just can't wait!

Here is the start of a game that could be written down using this code. The white moves are in one column, the black moves are in another. Try making these moves on your chessboard.

Code checklist

WHITE

1. **e4** Pawn move
2. **Nf3** Piece move
3. **Bb5+** Check sign
4. **Bxc6+** Capture sign
5. **0-0** Castles king-side

Checkmate **Qh5++**
Castles queen-side **0-0-0**
Pawn queens **e8=Q**

BLACK

c5 Pawn move
d6 Pawn move
Nc6 Piece move
bxc6 Pawn capture

Warming up

CHECK • CAPTURES

You now know the rules, but not how to win. To get you into shape you need to do some warming-up exercises. The first ones will be on checkmate, the ultimate object of the game.

Check

A check is when the king is under attack. A beginner usually reaches to move the king as soon as he is threatened. But hold on! There are other ways out. Maybe it's better to block or capture.

The black bishop moves down to b4 to check the king. You could move your king. But after that you wouldn't be able to castle.

32

Warming up

You could block by playing your pawn to c3. This would be better – but best of all would be to capture the bishop with your knight at d5.

Test yourself

1. OUT OF CHECK
In these exercises you are white and your king is in check. There is only one way out, either by MOVING the king, CAPTURING the enemy piece, or BLOCKING the check. (Answers on p120.)

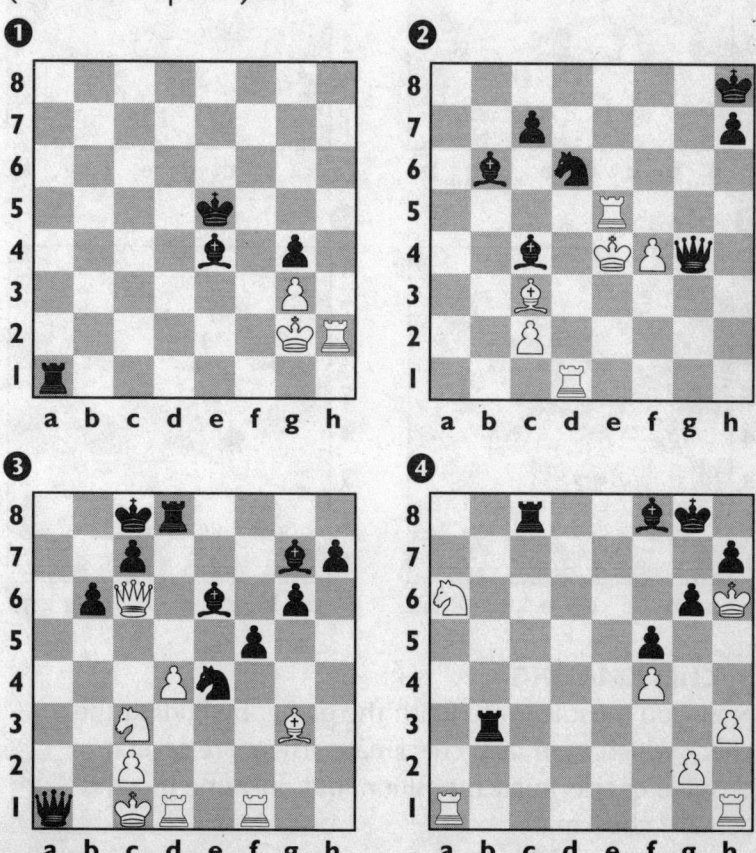

Warming up

2. HOW MANY CHECKS?

Find as many checks as you can for white on this move. In position one, some of the checks are **Qh6+**, **Bg3+** and **Nc4+**. There are others, too. None of the available checks is checkmate. (Answers on p120.)

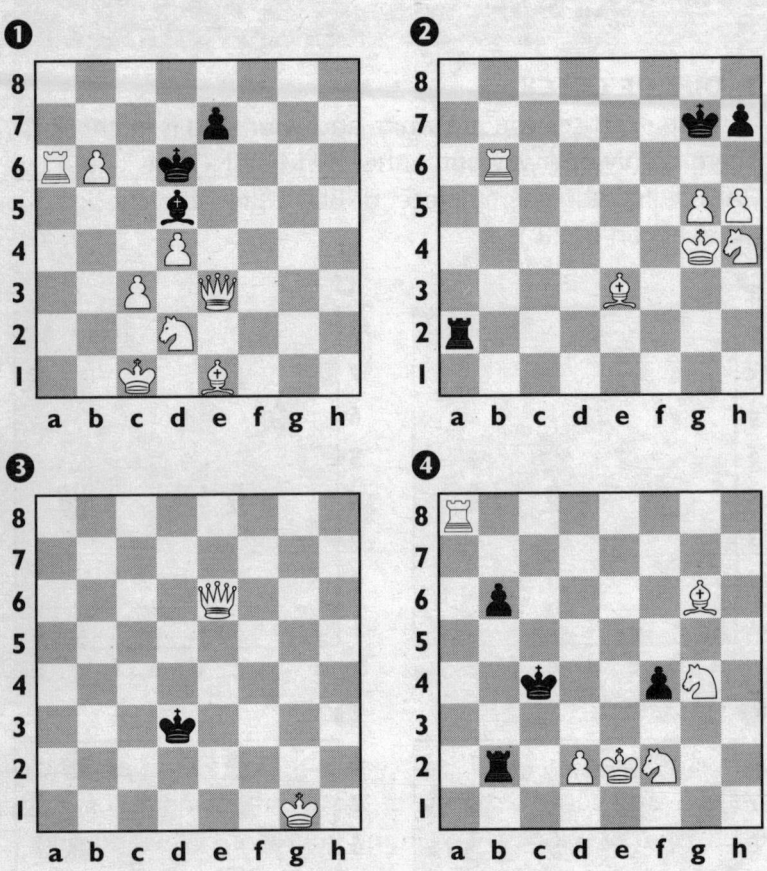

3. CHECKMATING

Now you must learn to finish the game, by finding the check which is, in fact, checkmate. There are several possible checks in each position, but only one move is actually checkmate.
(Answers on p120.)

Warming up

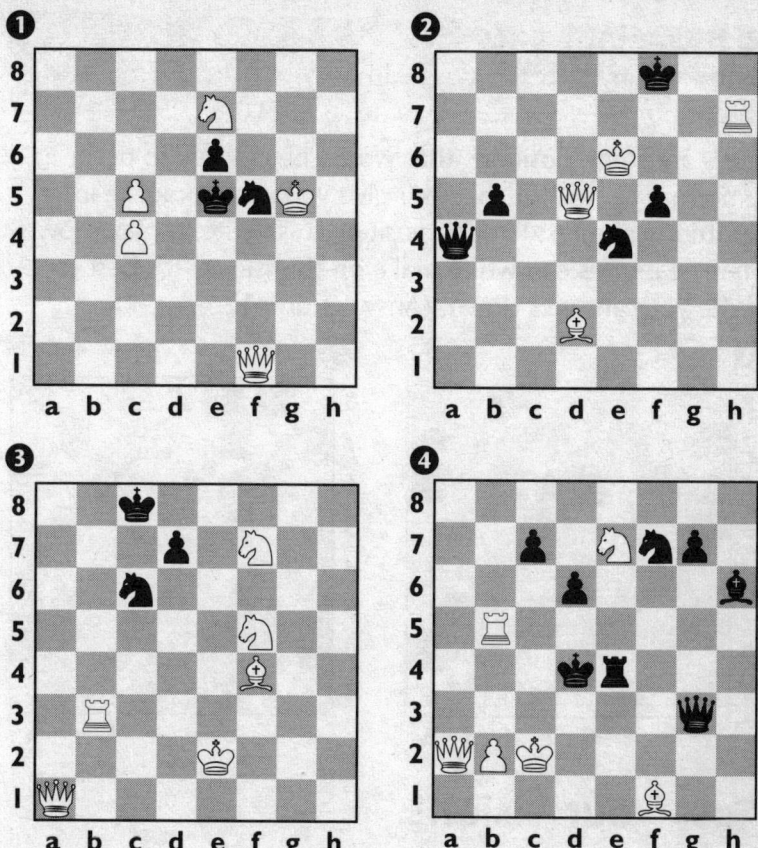

Captures

Although checkmate is the object of the game, other goals may have to come first. One of these is the winning of enemy pieces, while safeguarding your own. When playing against a skilful opponent, the loss of a single piece may spell defeat long before checkmate approaches. As a beginner, when you lose a piece you may think, "Never mind, I'll get it back later," or "I'll checkmate my opponent." In fact, instead of relying on good luck in the future, it would be better to learn simple capture skills, so that you don't lose the piece in the first place!

Warming up

Test yourself

Here are some positions that would be unlikely to occur in a normal game, but they will give you some practice in spotting captures. In each position it is white to play. How many captures can white make on this move? It's best to write your answers down. (Answers on p120.)

❶

❷

Test your vision!

Chess is a game of foresight. Have you ever seen players at a board, pondering a move? They are considering the possibilities: "If I choose that move, what will happen, and how will my opponent reply?"

You can get quite bogged down in all that thought, especially as there are more possibilities in chess than atoms in the universe! But chess is not only a game of thought – it is also one of decisions, so at some point you must stop thinking and make a move.

In these exercises, you look ahead to see whether a capture can be answered by a re-capture. There are already several

Warming up

possible outcomes, even with this simple forecasting. In the diagram below, white can make five different captures. Which one is the best?

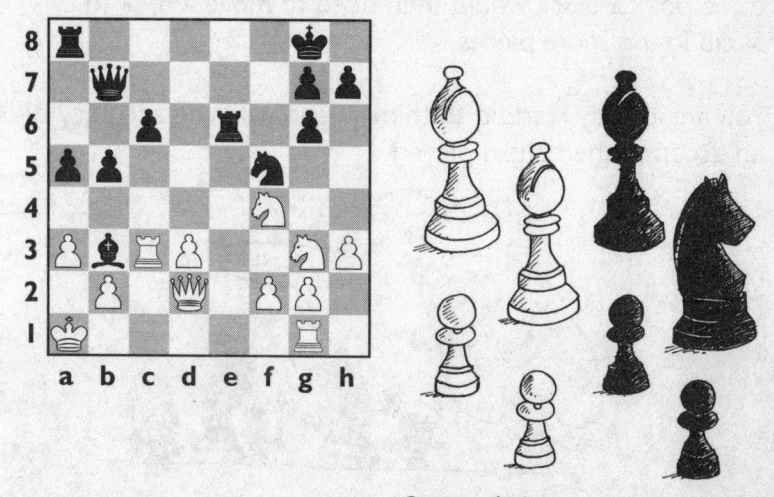

Captured pieces

In this position the points are quite level but, with the right capture, white can go ahead. Two captures are clearly bad:

- **Nxg6**, which loses a knight for a pawn after black recaptures by **hxg6**.
- **Rxc6**, a suicidal capture that gains you only one point but loses five after the re-capture **Rxc6** or **Qxc6**.

One capture is neutral:

- **Nxf5**. This exchanges knight for knight after the reply **gxf5**.

That leaves two captures: **Rxb3** or **Nxe6**. Which is the best? Apparently **Nxe6** is the best, for the black rook is worth five points. Many players would make this capture, showing their lack of foresight. In fact, it would only win two points,

Warming up

because the black bishop at b3 could step back and re-capture the knight, reducing the black loss to two points. The best capture is therefore **Rxb3**, when white wins a clear three points. Black would then need to move a rook to avoid losing more pieces.

You are already starting to think ahead with the accuracy of an accomplished chess player!

Test yourself

Now test yourself on the following positions. Which are the bad captures (that lose points after re-capture), the neutral captures (exchanges), and the good captures? Finally decide what your best move is. (Answers on p120–1.)

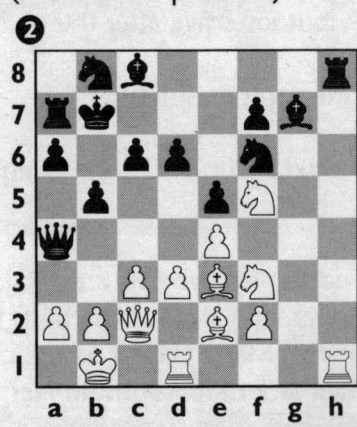

Warming up

"Every great player is a great analyst."
Mikhail Botvinnik

"The good player is always lucky."
José Raoul Capablanca

5. The tricky rules

CASTLING • STALEMATE • EN PASSANT
• TOUCH PIECE MOVE • RESIGNATION

Besides the basic rules of chess, you need to know about three tricky rules:

- castling
- stalemate
- en passant

The tricky rules

Castling

Well, you already know how to castle, but in case you've forgotten... the king moves TWO SQUARES and the rook jumps over.

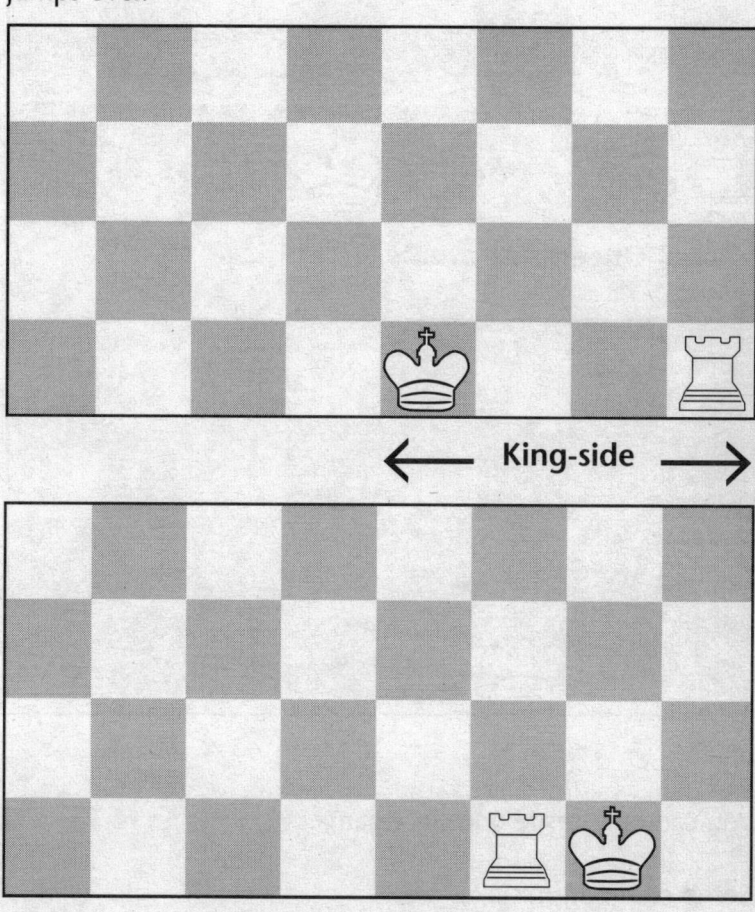

⟵ **King-side** ⟶

The tricky rules

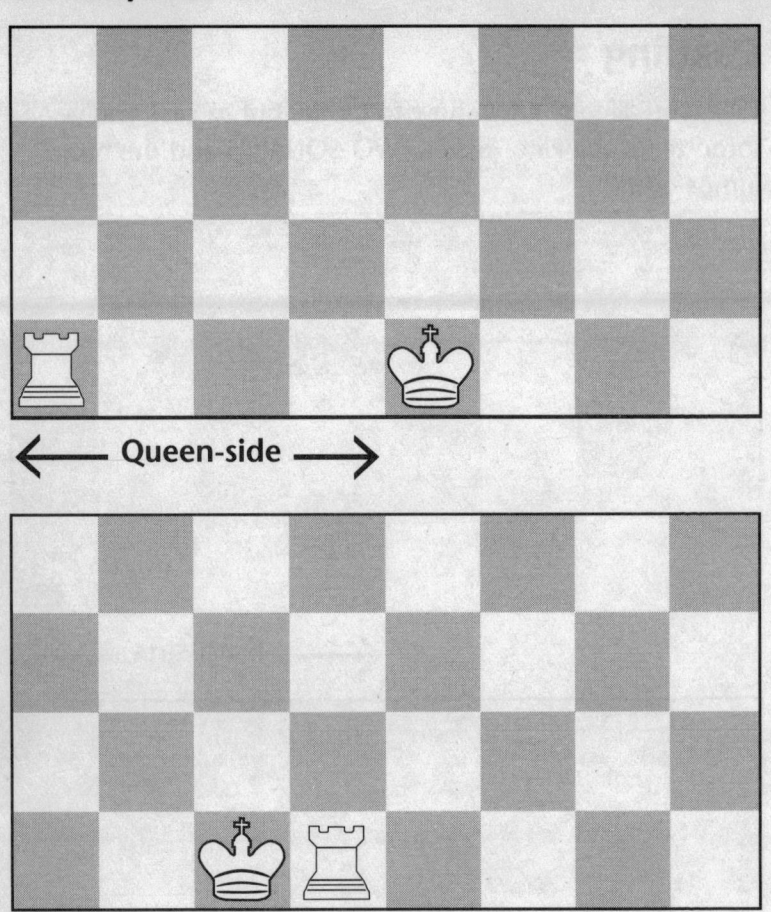

← **Queen-side** →

You can only castle once in a game.

Some common mistakes are:

- that the king and rook swap places. (They don't!)
- that the king moves THREE squares when he castles on the queen's side. (He doesn't. He moves only TWO squares, whichever side he goes.)

The tricky rules

Why castle?

- You take the king away from the centre of the battlefield.
- You tuck him behind a shield of pawns, where he is much safer. Try not to move these pawns up or you will lose your shield.

Sometimes you might decide to move up the pawn at the edge of the board to give the king an escape route if an enemy rook or queen invades your basement.

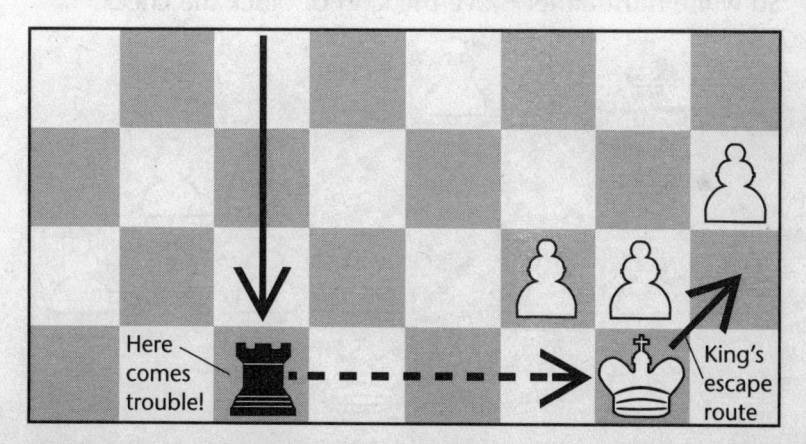

The tricky rules

When you can't castle

- If there are any pieces between the king and the rook.
- If the king or the rook have already moved. Castling must be the first move of the king and the rook.
- If the move means going into, out of or through check.

INTO CHECK

You can't castle here, as the king would land in check from the black queen.

OUT OF CHECK

Here the king is already in check from the black bishop. He can't get out of check by castling (it's against the rules). So white must either move the king or block the check.

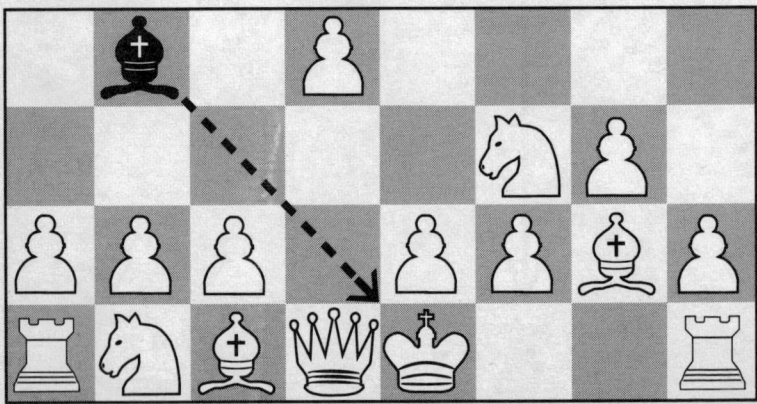

The tricky rules

THROUGH CHECK

You can't go through check. (Though thousands of players do, without noticing it!)

If the king tries to castle, he will pass over a square attacked by an enemy piece (the black rook). This is called 'castling through check' and it is strictly forbidden.

Board talk

A piece is en prise when it is placed where it can be captured or exchanged for a lower value piece. It's a mistake to leave a piece en prise!

The tricky rules

Stalemate

The aim of the game is to checkmate the enemy king, but a game can end in a draw if:

- both sides agree.
- they run out of pieces and haven't got enough pieces left to checkmate with.

But what if one side runs out of moves without being checkmated? It can happen.

Here the white king is boxed into a corner. Things look desperate, and the black king and queen are closing in to deliver checkmate. But suddenly white (to move) finds that there are no moves. The white pawn is paralysed, blocked by the enemy black pawn. And the white king can't move anywhere, because all the nearby squares are attacked by the enemy queen and king, and it is against the rules to move your king into check.

This sort of position is called stalemate, and it is declared a draw. White was lucky. White should have lost this game, but black carelessly suffocated white, leaving white no squares to move to before delivering the checkmating blow.

The tricky rules

Here black has avoided the stalemate trap. White's king is cornered, but still has two squares to move back and forth. When the king makes his move, the black queen can then checkmate (for example, by moving two squares sideways).

REMEMBER: CHECKMATE — DON'T SUFFOCATE!

Chess champs: Max Euwe (World Champion 1935–7)

Max Euwe was president of the International Chess Federation for many years. Late in life he noted: "I find that if I lose at chess, it doesn't hurt any more. And now I know I am done for."

The tricky rules

En passant

En passant is French for 'in passing'. En passant came in when modern chess began about 500 years ago. The new rules of chess allowed pawns to make an initial move of two squares, instead of just one. But there was a problem...

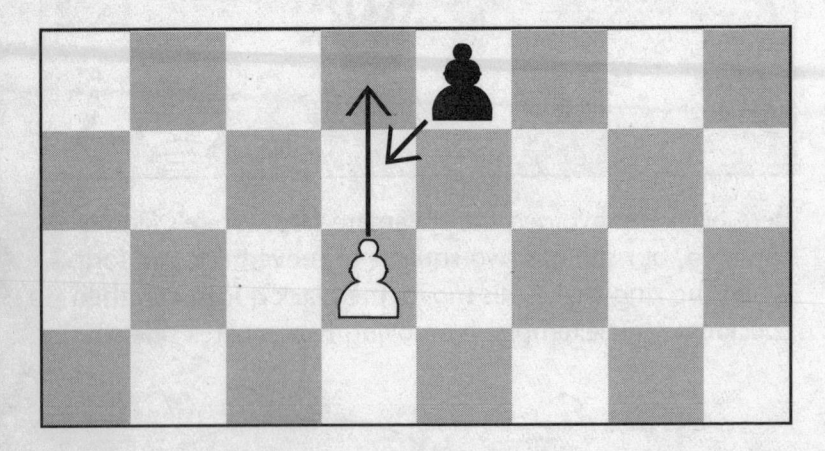

Under the old rules, a pawn moves up just one square and is captured by an enemy pawn. But under the new rules the pawn can move up two squares. This means that the enemy pawn can't capture it. Or does it?

This is where the en passant rule comes into action. This is what happens:

- A pawn moves two squares.
- It stands next to an enemy pawn.
- The enemy pawn can capture the first pawn as if it had moved only one square.
- The capture must be made immediately, or not at all.

The tricky rules

1. Before en passant

2. Pawn moves two squares and stands next to an enemy pawn.

3. Enemy pawn takes first pawn as if it had moved one square. Game opens up.

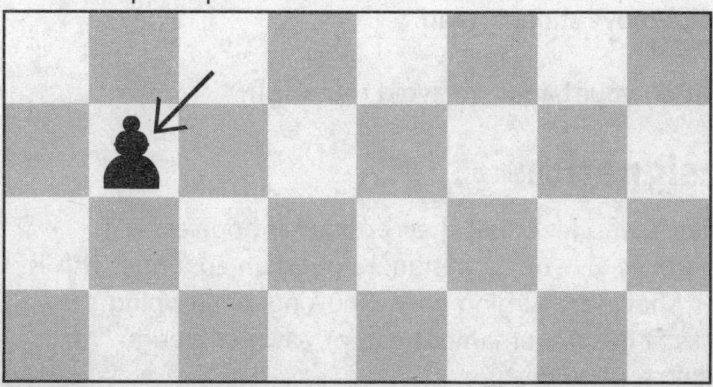

The tricky rules

En passant is *optional* – black can choose to capture or not. But once you decide not to make the capture, you can't do it later. The capture must be made immediately or not at all.

> **Chess champs: Mikhail Botvinnik (World Champion 1948–57, 1958–60, 1961–63)**
>
> *After World War II, the disciplined and dedicated players of the former Soviet Union were unstoppable. They were led by Mikhail Botvinnik. "Is Botvinnik invincible?" someone asked. "Of course not, nobody is, but he plays as though he is!" came the answer.*

Touch piece move

This rule is always used in chess tournaments, and it is a good idea to use it in friendly games too:

- If you touch a piece you must move it.
- If you touch an enemy piece you must capture it if you can.
- If you put a piece on a square and take your hand off it, that move should stand.

So sit on your hands, to avoid mistakes!

Resignation

A player who feels that their position is hopeless will sometimes give up, or resign, rather than continue. This is often shown by turning down the king, or stopping the clocks (if it is a tournament game), saying "I resign," or making a small gesture.

The tricky rules

Temperamental players sometimes sweep all the pieces off the board and storm out of the room. An angry king once brained his opponent with a wooden chessboard for beating him!

6 Into action

FOUR IDEAS • THE OPENING

You are now ready for your next battle. The board is set up. Your opponent sits opposite you. What is your approach? To play successfully, you must bear in mind four general ideas.

1. Maximum power – minimum exposure

Every piece aims for maximum power. In chess the power zone is the centre of the board. From the centre a piece attacks more squares, and its reach extends to all four corners of the board.

Into action

Think of the centre as being on the top of a hill. On the hilltop, you can see all around and you can reach any side of the hill quickly. So should we all rush into the centre as soon as possible? Well, no, because the more powerful you are, the weaker you are! Think of the most powerful people in the world: the President of the USA, rich millionaires, famous film stars. Are they safe? No – the President fears assassination, the millionaire may be kidnapped, the film star is mobbed by fans. They all need bodyguards. And the same goes for chess: if you put all your powerful pieces in the centre straightaway, they will be mobbed by smaller pieces. So approach the centre carefully. It's where you want to be, but start by putting your lower value pieces there first, and only risk your most valuable pieces when the danger from the enemy is less.

For example, the king (the most valuable piece) is at his most powerful in the centre, but would be checkmated very quickly if he moved there in the opening. His turn in the centre usually comes at the end of the game, when only puny pawns are left on the board.

Board talk

'Zugzwang' is a situation that often occurs near the end of a game. The player to move has to give way and make a losing move. They would rather not take a move at all, but that isn't allowed in chess. Zugzwang is a German word meaning 'compelled to move'.

Into action

2. Get your team to work together

You need as many pieces in action as quickly as possible. All these pieces need to guard each other, to work together against different enemy targets, and to work separately to cover different parts of the board. All this means teamwork, and good planning by the team manager – you!

3. Watch the enemy

The single most serious mistake is to forget about the enemy while you are thinking of your own plan. If you do that you will lose pieces because you will put your pieces where they can be captured, you will overlook enemy threats, and you may not even notice when your opponent makes mistakes. Guard your king, too. Poor defence can lose a game by checkmate after only two moves!!

4. Be aggressive

You want to win. Your opponent makes mistakes too! Don't resign too soon, and don't agree to draw until you've exhausted every winning chance.

Besides these general ideas, you should also use these special rules for the opening.

Into action

The rules of the opening

Follow these simple rules and you'll soon be playing the opening like a champion!

1 Put one or two pawns in the centre. Pawns are the weakest pieces and will help to scare away stronger enemy pieces. They will also shield your own pieces from the attentions of enemy pawns!

2 Bring out your knights and bishops near the centre. Get them off the back row, otherwise they will block your rooks. Bishops are at home in the centre, but as long-range pieces they can also function well away from the centre.

Three good placings for the versatile bishop:

Central (at c4)

Fianchetto (see page 56) at g2 striking across centre.

Into action

Off back row (on e2) allows castling.

Board talk

'Fianchetto' means 'at the edge of the board'. It is an Italian word meaning 'little flank'.

3   Move each piece once in the opening (except when capturing or avoiding capture).

Who has played better here?

White has begun badly by moving up a pawn to a4 and neglecting the centre; then white played a knight out to a3, b5, then back to c3 and finally home again to b1. Black has followed all our opening rules!

Into action

4 Castling. Get the king into safety by castling. After castling, keep some pawns back around the king.

5 Queen. Move her off the back row on to the second or third rank, but do not bring her into action too early. If you leave her on the back row, your rooks may be shut in.

6 Rooks. As rooks are high-value pieces, aim for maximum power and minimum exposure. Exchanging pawns opens up the game and gives the rooks scope. From the back row they can pound away against the enemy with very little danger to themselves.

7 Try to keep the balance of pieces even (unless you can actually win pieces) – exchange pawn for pawn, bishop for bishop or knight, rook for rook. In some openings, pawns are sacrificed to open up the game and to make the enemy lose time by capturing them but, otherwise, losing pawns and pieces is bad news.

Into action

> ### Board talk
>
> 'Sacrifice' is when you give up a piece or a pawn to win more pieces quickly, or to force checkmate.
>
> A 'gambit' is a sacrifice in the opening of the game, usually of a pawn, to improve your position – maybe by opening up the board, or to launch an attack. 'Gambit' literally means 'legpull'!

Capablanca v. Janowski

Now for a game that shows these rules in action. This is the opening of a game played between José Raoul Capablanca (white) and David Janowski (black) in New York, 1918.

Make these moves on your chessboard!

WHITE Capablanca	BLACK Janowski
1. d4	d5

(Rule 1: pawns in centre.)

2. Nf3	Nf6

(Rule 2: knights and bishops near centre.)

3. c4	e6

(Rule 1 again. But note that a pawn capture is now possible – the black pawn at d5 can take the white pawn at c4, or vice versa, and pawn captures open lines for

Into action

rooks (Rule 6). Eagle-eyed players will notice that black can capture the pawn at **c4** *for nothing*, but in this opening, called 'The Queen's Gambit', white can usually recover the pawn after **e3** and **Bxc4**.)

4. Bg5
(Rules 2 and 3: move each piece once in the opening.)

4. ...   **Nbd7**

(Why is this written **Nbd7**, not **Nd7**? This is because the knight on f6 (the 'f' knight) could also have gone to d7. In fact the knight at b8 (the 'b' knight) went there.)

5. e3   c6

6. Nbd2   Be7

7. Bd3   dxc4

8. Nxc4
(Rule 3: move each piece once, except when capturing or avoiding capture. Capablanca (white) evens up the points by recapturing a pawn.)

8. ...   **0-0**

9. 0-0
(Rule 4: castle your king into safety.)

9. ...   **c5**

10. Rc1
(Rule 6: place rooks where they are not blocked by their own pawns. The knight at c4 is in the rook's way, but a knight can move off a file and a pawn cannot.)

10. ...   **b6**

(Black plays **b6** to get the bishop at c8 out into the game (Rule 2).)

10.   **Rc1**

Into action

> 11. **Qe2**
> (Rule 5: take the queen off the back row (to get her out of the way of the rooks) but not too far forward (to avoid exposing her). The second or third rank is best.)
> 11. ... **Bb7**
> 12. **Rfd1**
> (Rule 6: place rooks on open lines. The pawns at c5 and d4 may be exchanged, and then the road will be clear for the rook.)

One quick way of measuring your success in the opening is to count how many moves it will take you to 'connect rooks' (set up a position where the rooks guard each other along the back row).

Now you've learned how to play the opening. Try out your new-found knowledge in your next game of chess!

Into action

Chess champs: Bobby Fischer (World Champion 1972-5)

Bobby Fischer was a grandmaster at the age of 15, and his tantrums and on-off tactics always made headline news of his matches. He turned down a million dollars to play for the world title declaring: "No-one's going to make a nickel out of me!"

Chess without tears

Mistakes are easy to make in chess, but to avoid the worst ones, try the simple thinking method in this checklist:

Your opponent moves...

1 Can he/she capture anything?

2 Can you capture anything?

3 What is your best move?

4 Write it down, before moving.

5 Think about it again – is it really safe?

6 If not, cross it out and choose another move.

7 If it is safe, make your move.

7. Winning ways

Scholar's Mate • Dawn Raider
• Diagonals • Giuoco Piano
• Copy cats • Castled king

Your chess database is filling up – the rules, capturing, checkmating and opening play. Now for some special tips to help you win.

1. Scholar's Mate

Try this out – it's guaranteed to beat most people! Every chessplayer needs to know about these pitfalls, if only to avoid them. Scholar's Mate is the classic four-move checkmate. If your opponent knows it, he or she is not a beginner!

Winning ways

WHITE	BLACK
1. e4	e5
2. Bc4	Bc5
3. Qh5	

(The moment of truth. Does black know how to defend?)

3. ... Nf6

(Not this time! White finishes with a snappy checkmate.)

4. Qxf7++

(Game over.)

Why does Scholar's Mate trap so many victims? I think one reason is that players do not believe they can be beaten so quickly, so they are caught out before they have even begun to think. The second reason is that all the play is on the diagonals, used effectively by queen and bishop. Diagonal moves are much harder to get used to than up-and-down and sideways moves (like the rooks), so these threats are often missed.

Winning ways

Let's have an action replay of this game.

WHITE	BLACK
1. e4	e5
2. Bc4	Bc5
3. Qh5	

(Stop! How would you defend as black?)

3. ... Qe7

(Simple as that. Black defends the pawn at f7, and white cannot checkmate any more. If white plays...)

4. Qxf7+   Qxf7
5. Bxf7+   Kxf7

(...black emerges two points ahead.)

Another good defence is:
3. ...   Qf6

Chess champs: Anatoly Karpov (World Champion 1975–85)

Anatoly Karpov was so thin as a teenager that experts doubted that he would have the stamina to become World Champion. They were wrong. Karpov had a will of iron, summed up in his comment, "I always have to be first."

Winning ways

Variations on Scholar's Mate

The zigzag attack

WHITE	BLACK
1. e4	e5
2. Bc4	Bc5
3. Qh5	g6
4. Qxe5+	

(At least black doesn't get checkmated.)

4. ...	Qe7
5. Qxh8	

(But black does lose a rook.)

The ambush

This is the most complicated version of Scholar's Mate.

WHITE	BLACK
1. e4	e5
2. Bc4	Bc5
3. Qh5	Nh6

(Black guards the f7 square with the knight. White now has a cunning plan – to ambush the knight at h6 with the white bishop, at present hiding behind the pawn at d2.)

4. d4	Bxd4
5. Bxh6	gxh6
6. Qxf7++	

(Same old story!)

Winning ways

2. Dawn Raider

This is another rapid opening attack, which again targets the weak square at f7.

WHITE	BLACK
1. e4	e5
2. Nf3	Nc6
3. Bc4	Nf6

(Of course, black does not necessarily play these moves, but they are quite common, so here is how you carry out your raid.)

4. Ng5
(Aiming for f7.)

4. ... h6
(Black hasn't woken up yet!)

5. Nxf7
(This is a perfect example of a knight fork – and black walked straight into it! The knight at f7, guarded by the bishop at c4, threatens both the queen at d8 and the rook at h8, and white will win one or the other.)

5. ... Qe7
(Best of a bad job!)

6. Nxh8
(White is now six points ahead.)

Winning ways

Computer chess

The top chess computer is the IBM main frame known as Deep Blue. It beat World Champion Garry Kasparov in a short match in 1996. Computers can look at 2,000,000 moves a second, but humans still have the edge on planning... and they can always turn the computer off!

3. Grab that opportunity!

In football, when a striker sees a defender is in the wrong place, the striker quickly uses the opportunity to score. But the chance must be seized at once, before the gap is closed.

The deadly diagonal

In chess, there is an opportunity when your opponent weakens a diagonal leading to the king. You can often get a checkmate or a big advantage out of this.

WHITE	BLACK
1. e4	f6
2. d4	g5
3. Qh5++	

3. Qh5++

You have reached checkmate already because the pawns cannot block the diagonal. This is your pattern.

Winning ways

The exact moves shown on page 67 will hardly ever turn up, but similar situations do and it's up to you to spot them! For example:

WHITE	BLACK
1. e4	e5
2. Nf3	f6

(Black guards the pawn at e5. There doesn't seem to be anything wrong with that, but...)

3. Nxe5
(White seizes the chance!)

3. ... fxe5

4. Qh5+
(Now black is in a mess. If black plays 4. g6, black is going to be zigzagged (see page 65) by the moves 5. Qxe5+ and 6. Qxh8. On the other hand, if black's king takes a walk, it could be just as dangerous.)

4. ...	Ke7
5. Qxe5+	Kf7
6. Bc4+	Kg6
7. Qf5+	Kh6
8. d4+	g5
9. h4	

(Black's king is suffering a non-stop barrage of attacking moves. It's unlikely the king will survive this treatment.)

Winning ways

And now another example from a game played by José Raoul Capablanca. This game took place in a simultaneous contest – Capablanca was playing about 30 players at the same time, but he thought so quickly that he managed it with ease!

Capablanca knew exactly what to do because he recognised the pattern.

The diagonal was open and Capablanca went straight on:

WHITE	BLACK

11. Qh5+

(How would you continue if black played 11. **g6** here? The most successful attack would be 12. **Bxg6+ hxg6** 13. **Qxg6+ Ke7** 14. **Rxf6 Nxf6** 15. **Qg7+ Kd6** 16. **Nf7+**, winning black's queen with a knight fork.)

What actually happened was:

11. ...   **Ke7**

12. **Bxh7**   **Nf8**

(A new weakness has appeared at g6, and black defends the square against the threat of a knight fork by **Ng6+**. Now Capablanca rattled off his seven-move checkmate.)

13. **Qf7+**   **Kd6**

14. **Nc4+**   **dxc4**

15. **Ne4+**   **Kd5**

Winning ways

16. **Rf5+**	**Kxe4**
17. **Re1+**	**Kxd4**
18. **c3+**	**Kd3**
19. **Rd5++**	

19. Rd5++

Fantastic!

The final check is a double check (from rook and bishop). White has far fewer pieces on the board, but the attack was so ferocious that black never stood a chance.

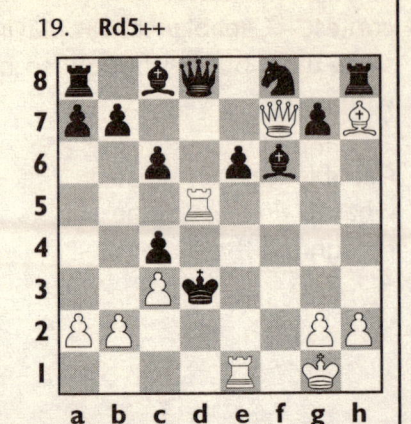

Record breakers

The youngest grandmaster is Etienne Bacrot of France, who, at 14, beat the record set by Michael Adams of Britain by three years!

Winning ways

Test yourself

1 You are WHITE. It looks like you are in trouble here, your bishop on g3 is trapped by the advancing black pawns. But suddenly you remember the deadly diagonal, and you find a way out. What is it? (Answers on page 121.)

2 Here you are BLACK, and you are pondering where to move your knight, which is attacked by the pawn at d3. But then you see something else. What is it? (Answers on page 121.)

Straight down the middle

Some openings try to get the pawns out of the centre as soon as possible so you can attack the enemy with rooks and queens. This one is called the Giuoco Piano, and it works like a dream!

Board talk

'Giuoco Piano' is a famous chess opening, invented by the Italians. It means literally 'quiet game'.

Winning ways

WHITE	BLACK
1. e4	e5
2. Nf3	Nc6
3. Bc4	Bc5
4. c3	
4. ...	Nf6
5. d4	exd4
6. cxd4	Bb4+

4. ...   Nf6

7. Nc3

7. Nc3

The two pawns side by side on the central squares d4 and e4 give white 'midfield domination', because the pawns also attack four squares in black's half of the board. Black acts swiftly to destroy one of the pawns, and wins the battle in the centre.

7. ...   Nxe4

(Black can do this because the white knight at c3 is powerless and pinned.)

8. 0-0

(Black has snapped at the bait, the 'e' file is now open – let's get a rook on to it!)

8. ...   Nxc3

(A wary opponent would have captured the knight with the bishop and then stabilised the position with pawn to d5, keeping the 'e' file closed with the knight. But black hasn't seen this one before.)

Winning ways

9. bxc3   Bxc3

(Two pawns ahead and a rook in prospect, black is asking "Can chess really be this easy?" It isn't!)

10. Ba3

A sly move to trap the black king in the centre (you can't castle through check (see page 45).)

10. ...   Bxa1

(Black takes another valuable piece)

11. Re1+

(The trap is sprung. Desperately black looks around and sees 'no exit' signs plastered all over the board. It's too late... black should never have taken that last rook. Now black has to give it all back and lose the queen as well.)

11. ...   Ne7

12. Bxe7   Qxe7

13. Rxe7+   Kxe7

14. Qxa1

King in the middle, rooks and bishop inactive on their starting squares, and the white pieces all poised to attack. Defeat for black is almost certain.

Now you know the pattern, let's see it in action in another position.

Winning ways

The copy cat trap

This can be used against those annoying people who copy everything that you do.

WHITE	BLACK
1. e4	e5
2. Nf3 (Copy cat!)	Nf6
3. Nxe5 (Copy cat!)	Nxe4

4. Qe2

(Now black stops and has a think. If black plays 4. **Qe7** (copying), white could play 5. **Qxe4** and then black **Qxe5** loses the queen to 6. **Qxe5**+! Not liking this, black decides to save the knight.)

4. ...   Nf6

5. Nc6+

The discovered check wins the black queen, because how ever black gets out of check, the white knight will take the black queen next move.

4. Qe2

5. Nc6+

Black tried to copy white, but white knew better, and used the pattern of attack down the central line to win the queen.

Winning ways

Chess champs: Garry Kasparov (World Champion 1985–)

Garry Kasparov is fitter, stronger, and works harder than any other World Champion. He plays to win, especially with black, using his super-aggressive King's Indian and Sicilian Najdorf variations. He was planning to retire in the year 2000, but now thinks he's getting better as he gets older.

Winning ways

Test yourself

1. Black captured a pawn here with **Qxe4**. Was black correct? (Answers on page 121.)

2. You can win in two moves here. (Clue: remember, straight down the middle!) (Answers on page 121.)

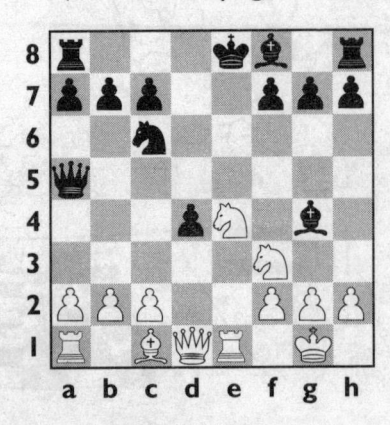

3. Black's king is safe and castled, white's is not. Now, using your queen, rook and bishop, checkmate white in five moves (every move is check, so white hasn't got much choice!). (Answers on page 121.)

Winning ways

> **Board talk**
>
> *A weak pawn is a pawn that is hard to defend. This may be because it is cut off from other pawns, too far behind, or stacked up with other pawns. Careful – pawns are easy targets!*

The castled king

A castled king is much safer than a king in the middle. To get to the king, you must first overcome his defenders, the pawns. So weaken! Invade! Destroy!

Winning ways

Here is an example from a game between Belitzmann (white) and Akiba Rubinstein (black).

WHITE	BLACK
Belitzmann	Rubinstein

12. ... Qh4
(The threat of checkmate by ... Qxh2++ forces a pawn to advance.)

13. g3 Qh3
(Getting closer.)

14. c3
(White sees that he is not in danger of checkmate by ... Qg2 because both his knights guard that square. So he decides to attack, starting with the knight at d4.)

14. ... h5
(Black does not bother to move the piece, but begins a brilliant plan to open up the file for his rooks.)

15. cxd4 h4

16. Qe2
(White sees that the line is about to be opened, and with this cunning move hopes to keep the vital h2 square guarded. If black now plays 16. ... hxg3 17. fxg3 by a miracle checkmate is avoided, because the white queen now defends the h2 pawn.)

16. Qe2

78

Winning ways

A brilliant defensive move needs a brilliant attack to secure victory. Can you see how Rubinstein checkmated from the last diagram in only three moves? (Answer on page 121.)

Test yourself

1. White is ready to checkmate on h7 with queen and bishop. But there's just one drawback – the knight at f6 guards the vital square. How does white solve the problem? (Answer on page 121.)

2. Here white has another way to make use of the idea of checkmate at h7. How does he win a rook or checkmate after his next move? (Answer on page 121.)

Winning ways

3 White has got her queen lined up against the g7 square, but she needs reinforcements. What do you suggest? (Answer on page 121.)

4 Black has castled – can you bring up an extra attacking unit and set up unanswerable threats? (Answer on page 121.)

Board talk

International Master is a title awarded by the World Chess Federation. England's Luke McShane got the title at age 13, and is now going for grandmaster!

8 Winning by force

LAWN MOWER MATE
• QUEEN MATE • BOX MATE

SUPERIOR FORCE →

In chess, superior force wins. If you have captured more pieces than your opponent, either due to your opponent's mistakes or your own good play, you have a clear path to victory. At this point, you need to know about the three basic checkmates.

1. The Lawn Mower Mate

The Lawn Mower Mate is done with two rooks against a king, although the same pattern can be used with a queen and a rook together, too.

81

Winning by force

The black king is the last piece left, but black is still hoping for a stalemate. How can white checkmate black from this position, in fewer than ten moves?

The first thing to remember is that white mustn't just check black. If white keeps on putting black in check, the game will be called a draw (by 'perpetual' check).

White needs two ideas: the fence and the lawn mower. The plan is to force the black king to the edge of the board. White's first task is to make a fence.

WHITE	BLACK
1. Ra4	

(White does not check but with one move cuts the board in half. The rook fires along the fourth row, and the black king cannot pass over this line, because he would be moving into check. So this is the fence.)

1. ...   Ke5

(The black king walks along the fence, looking for a way out.)

2. Rh1

(You will see the point of this move in a minute.)

2. ...   Kf5

3. Rh5+

(This second idea is the lawn mower. The rook checks along the rank, and forces the black king back towards the edge of the board. Because the other rook is still guarding the fence, the king cannot step into the middle of the board. Because of the way the rooks seem to mow the board into neat strips,

Winning by force

this checkmate is called the lawn mower.)

3. ... Kg6

(Black steps back but is still not giving up without a fight. Black has found a weakness in the fence, and with the next move intends to capture the rook. What does white do here?)

4. Rb5

(Excellent move! The black king is too close, so white whizzes his rook over to the other side of the board, far away from the feeble king, who now has to trudge back towards the rooks to find a hole in the fence.)

4. ... Kf6

(Back goes the king. But now the rooks are in a position to finish him off.)

5. Ra6+

(The rooks swap roles. Earlier, this rook was the fence and the other one was the lawn mower. Now this rook mows the lawn, while the other guards the fence.)

5. ... Kf7

6. Rb7+ Ke8

7. Ra8++

(The rooks checkmate well below the target of ten moves.)

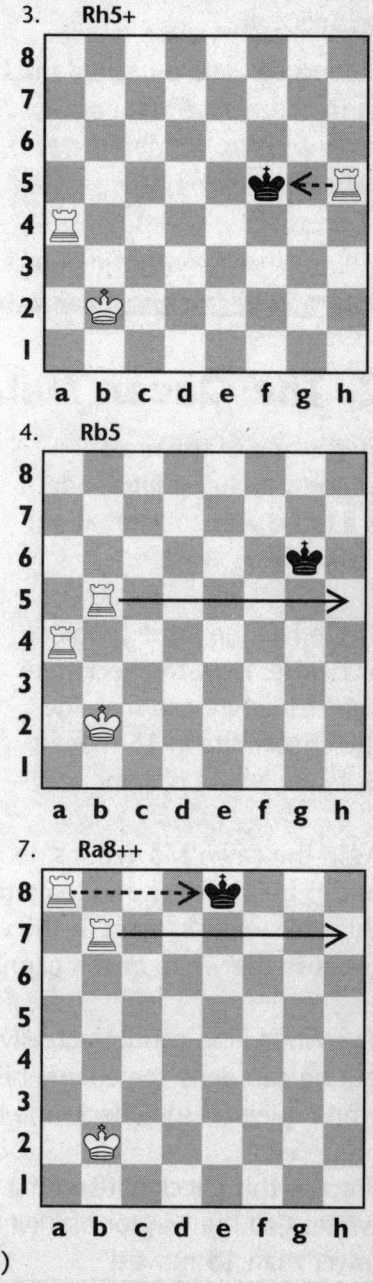

3. Rh5+

4. Rb5

7. Ra8++

Winning by force

Board talk

A chess clock is a double clock which times the moves of both players, so they do not take too long. Chess clocks were introduced at the beginning of the 20th century, when time limits were about 12 moves per hour. Things have speeded up since then – regular tournament time limits today are 20 moves an hour!

2. The Queen Mate

This is one of the most important checkmates, and it is a good way to learn about stalemate as well!

White has the same problem as before. How to checkmate black? If white can manage the checkmate in 15 moves or fewer, white is doing well.

As in the Lawn Mower, it's no good just checking. White has to build fences and force the enemy on to the edge. In this case white's 'team' is the white king and queen, because the white queen cannot checkmate on her own.

The white king cannot actually do any checking himself, but he can deny the enemy his squares and guard the white queen if she checks the black king at close range.

Practise this checkmate with a friend, taking turns to be white. Call it a win for black if white can't checkmate in fewer than 15 moves!

Winning by force

Here are some mating positions to aim for.

Queen on top. The queen is guarded by the white king and delivers a close checkmate.

Queen sideways. The queen checks along the edge, while the white king prevents any escape.

Winning by force

Starting from the position on p84, white can play:

WHITE	BLACK
1. **Qf3**	

(White immediately boxes the black king in. The king cannot stray beyond the boundary lines marked out in the diagram.)

1. ...	**Kd4**

(Black must try to stay in the middle.)

2. **Kb2**	**Ke5**
3. **Kc3**	

(The white king arrives on the scene. Black cannot now move into the central d4 square.)

3. ...	**Ke6**
4. **Kd4**	

(White is now dominant in the centre and can chase the black king wherever he moves.)

4. ...	**Kd6**
5. **Qf6+**	

(A Lawn Mower type check drives the king ever closer to the edge.)

5. ...	**Kd7**
6. **Kd5**	**Kc7**
7. **Qc6+**	**Kd8**

(Black has been driven to the edge of the board. But black sets a last desperate trap. What move would you choose as white? The answer is on page 122.)

Winning by force

3. The Box Mate

This is the checkmate by king and rook against king. The forces here are not as powerful as in the Lawn Mower and Queen mates, so they need to work closely together to overcome the enemy king's resistance.

Once again the black king starts off in the best defensive position in the middle of the board. White's job is to get him on to the edge of the board. White starts by approaching with the king.

Winning by force

WHITE	BLACK
1. Kb2	Kd5
2. Kc3	Ke5

(Next white links the king up with the rook.)

3. Rh4	Kd5
4. Rd4+	Ke5

(This is the first position to aim for – you can see that black's king has been boxed in to one quarter of the board. By itself, the rook cannot control the black king, because the king can always attack the rook diagonally. That is why the rook needs to be supported by his own king to make the box watertight.)

Having set up the box, white must now gradually make it smaller. There are three types of move to do this:

- Making the box smaller with the rook.
- Bringing the king closer.
- Playing a waiting move with the rook.

Winning by force

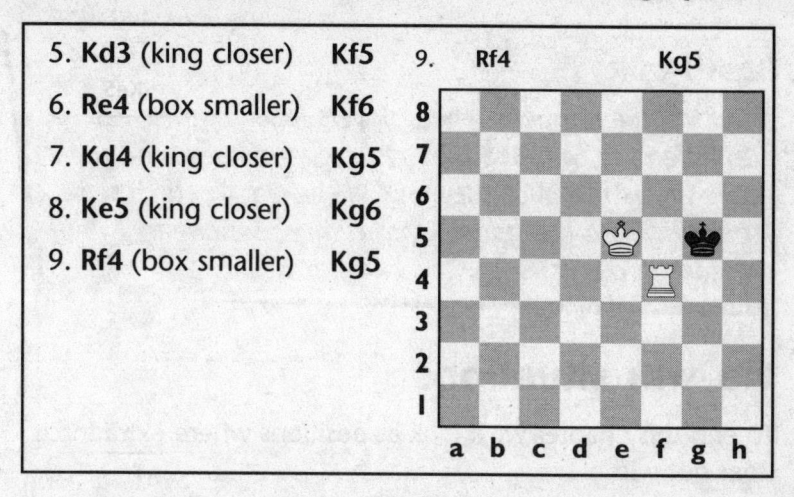

5. **Kd3** (king closer)	**Kf5**	9. Rf4 Kg5
6. **Re4** (box smaller)	**Kf6**	
7. **Kd4** (king closer)	**Kg5**	
8. **Ke5** (king closer)	**Kg6**	
9. **Rf4** (box smaller)	**Kg5**	

Now white can neither make the box smaller, nor move the king closer. So try this:

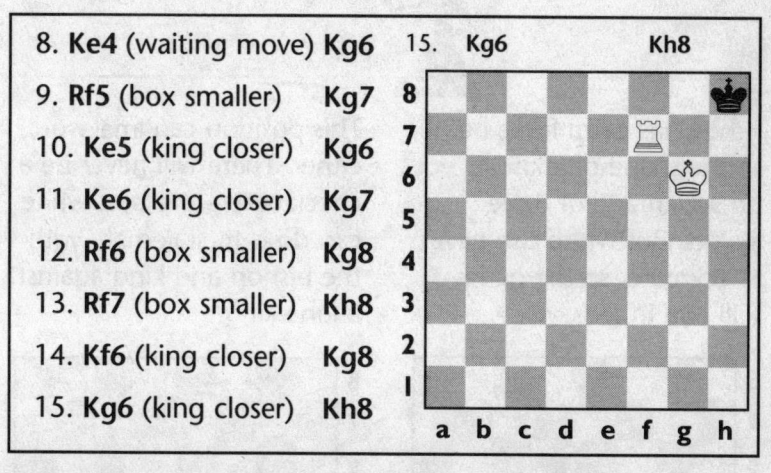

8. **Ke4** (waiting move)	**Kg6**	15. Kg6 Kh8
9. **Rf5** (box smaller)	**Kg7**	
10. **Ke5** (king closer)	**Kg6**	
11. **Ke6** (king closer)	**Kg7**	
12. **Rf6** (box smaller)	**Kg8**	
13. **Rf7** (box smaller)	**Kh8**	
14. **Kf6** (king closer)	**Kg8**	
15. **Kg6** (king closer)	**Kh8**	

Now black is down to a box of only two squares, and it is time to take stock. It's no use continuing to make the box smaller and if white plays 16. **Rg7**, it will be stalemate. Instead white can win with 16. **Rf8** checkmate.

If the black king were on g8 instead of h8, white would first play **Rf6**, then **Rf8++**.

Winning by force

> **Board talk**
>
> *Time trouble happens when players leave themselves too little time to make their remaining moves, and then have to rush to beat the clock. If the clock beats them, they may lose the game, even if they're a queen ahead on points!*

No win situations

To end this chapter we'll look at positions where extra force does not win.

White has extra force here in the shape of a knight – an advantage of three points. But white can never checkmate, so the game will end in a draw.

This position can't be won either. There will never be a checkmate – the best white can do is to stalemate with the bishop and king against a lone king.

90

Winning by force

What about this position? Do you think white can win it?
(Answer on page 122.)

Record breakers

The top woman player is Judith Polgar, ranked number 17 in the world. She beat ex-World Champion, Anatoly Karpov, in a match in 1998.

9 Getting the edge

• IMPROVING YOUR GAME •

'Improvement comes through refinement.'

This means that hitting your opponent over the head is not always the best way to win an argument! If there is no checkmate, and no way to win pieces, you can still build up your advantage by:

- placing your pieces better, nearer the centre, or nearer the enemy king.
- controlling important squares with your pieces and pawns, especially centre squares.
- weakening enemy pawns, or the pawns around the king.

Getting the edge

Here is a classic example from José Raoul Capablanca, who uses many of these ideas in one game. He was playing Rudolf Spielmann at New York in 1927.

If we look at this position, it is hard to see who is better. The points are level, black's king is safe, and white will soon castle. But black's bishop at c8, and central pawns, are both on the same coloured squares. This means that black is strong on squares of one colour (white) but weak on squares of the other colour. Put it another way: if you had lots of horses and carts and controlled the roads, you might still be defeated by an opponent who used the rivers and canals.

WHITE	BLACK
Capablanca	Spielmann

12. **0-0**   a6

13. **Rfe1**
(White prepares to play a pawn to e4. We know why pawn exchanges are made.)

13. ...   **Qe6**
(Black unpins the knight, which was trapped by the white bishop at g5. Black is now ready to capture the white pawn if it foolishly moves to e4.)

14. **Nd2**
(White renews the threat of playing the pawn to e4.)

14. ...   **b5**

Getting the edge

15. Qa5
(The white queen settles on a dark square where the black pawn and bishop, marooned on white squares, cannot attack her.)

15 ... Ne4
(Finally, black plugs up the e4 square, and puts paid to white's attempts to play e4. It is clear that the white rook will not get into the game from e1.)

16. Nxe4 dxe4

17. a4
(White makes a pawn thrust to break up the chain on the queen side. It would not be a good idea now for black to capture by 17. ... **bxa4**, since after 18. **Rxa4**, the pawn at c4 would be on its own and difficult to defend.)

17. ... Qd5
(The players are matching each other blow for blow.
But now Capablanca unleashes the winning combination.)

18. axb5
(White is prepared to lose the bishop at g5 in order to destroy black's position on the queen side.)

18. ... Qxg5
(Black has no alternative but to make the intended capture, since if black plays 18. ... **axb5**, black loses a rook after 19. **Qxa8 Qxa8** 20. **Rxa8**.

Getting the edge

19. Bxe4	Rb8
20. bxa6	

20. bxa6

Black's defences have crumbled. Capablanca's pawn at a6, ready to queen in two moves, gives him a winning advantage. White used central play, line opening and better placed pieces to overcome his opponent.

Board talk

The grading system (or ranking system) is a way of ranking players by strength (see page 112). Chess has one of the most sophisticated ranking systems in the world. Depending how well you play against other players, you gain a ranking which goes up and down when you win or lose matches.

10 Winning by tactics

THE FORK • THE PIN • DISCOVERED ATTACK

In the early part of this book we looked at simple capturing ideas, but as we moved on, many of the games showed complicated movements lasting for several moves, needing good calculating skills. This part of chess is called tactics. We are now going to look at some of the most simple tactical ideas.

The fork
(also called the double attack)

Black's knight attacks two or more pieces at once, ensuring that black will win one of them. This is one of the best ways to win pieces.

Winning by tactics

The pin

The stronger piece is shielded by the weaker piece, and if the weaker piece moves out of the way, the stronger one is captured. In the diagram, the knight at f6 is pinned by the bishop at g5. If the knight moves away, white can capture the black queen.

Only rooks, bishops and queens can pin, whereas all pieces can fork. Here are three ways to use the power of the pin:

The pinned pieces are both worth more than the pinner. A simple capture wins pieces. In this diagram, we're only four moves into the game, and black has hit the jackpot. Black's move 4. ... **Bb4** pins and wins the white queen.

The pinned piece is held in place while other pieces attack it, allowing white to capture and win points. The rook at e1 pins the bishop at e7 against the black rook. Instead of capturing the bishop immediately, white plays a bishop to g5. No black piece can come to the rescue of the e7 bishop, and black must lose pieces.

97

Winning by tactics

A pinned piece does not defend. White carelessly plays 1. **Qxd5** here, thinking she has won a knight, because her queen is guarded by the white knight at c3. But after black replies 1. ... **Qxd5**, white realises that she has lost her queen, because the knight at c3 is pinned and cannot re-capture.

Pro quote

"Chess is 99% tactics."

Richard Teichmann

The discovered attack

The discovered attack includes the discovered check and the double check. It is rather like a free kick in football. One piece moves out of the way of another, and discovers (or uncovers) an attack from the piece behind. To inflict maximum damage with your 'free kick', the piece moving out of the way should also attack something.

Winning by tactics

Here the black rook and knight are lined up against the white king. Black uncovers a check against the white king by playing the knight to f4. At the same time, the black knight threatens the white queen at h5. After white has moved out of check, black captures the queen.

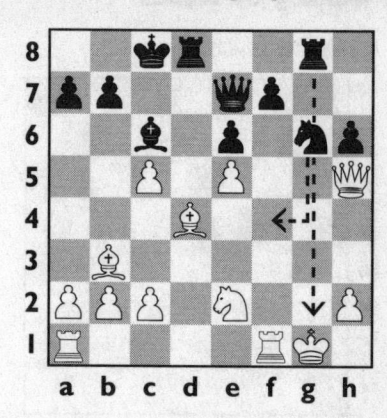

Test yourself

Try testing yourself with these diagrams.
(Answers are on page 123.)

Forks

In each position one side can make a fork that will win points or end in checkmate. Find the crushing move and the two threats.

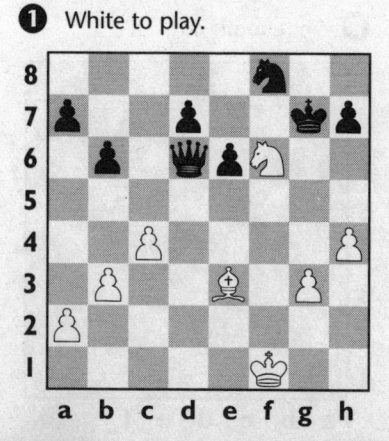

❶ White to play.

❷ White to play.

99

Winning by tactics

3 White to play.

4 White to play.

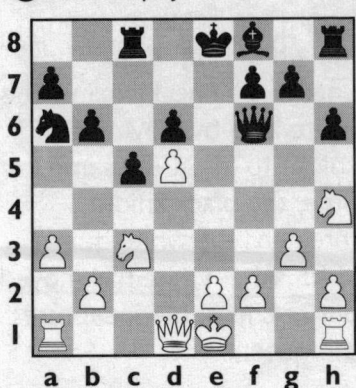

5 White to play.

6 White to play.

7 Black to play.

8 White to play.

Winning by tactics

Pins

Find the pinned piece in each position. Attack the pinned piece so that you can win points on your next move. (Answers are on page 123.)

❶ Black to move and attack a pinned piece.

❷ White to move and attack a pinned piece.

❸ White to move and attack a pinned piece.

❹ White to move and attack a pinned piece. Make sure it is a legal move!

Winning by tactics

5 White uses a pin to win points.

6 Black wins three points. How?

7 Should black take a rook, or is there a better move?

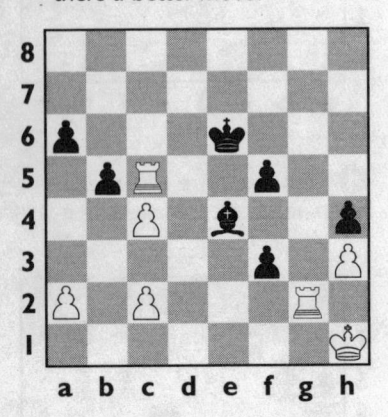

8 White mates in two moves. The pin helps.

Winning by tactics

Discovered check

In each position, white or black has a devastating discovered check, or a discovery that wins points. (Answers on page 123.)

❶ Black to play.

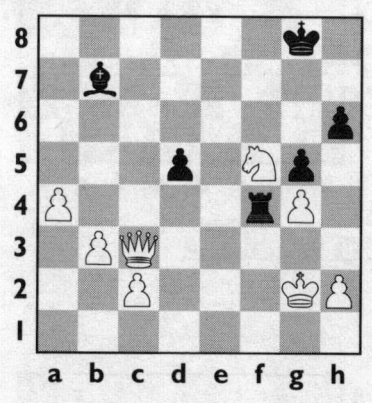

❷ Black to play.

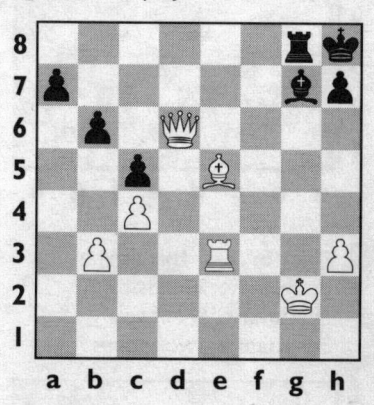

❸ Black to play.

❹ Black to play.

103

Winning by tactics

5 White to play.

6 White to play.

7 Black to play. This time a double check leads to checkmate. See if you can mate in two moves.

8 White to play.

Winning by tactics

Mating attacks

Terminate your opponent in just one move! The queen is the strongest attacking piece. In these positions, the white queen delivers the mating blow in one move.
(Answers on page 124.)

❶ White to play.

❷ White to play.

❸ White to play.

❹ White to play.

105

Winning by tactics

5 White to play.

6 White to play.

7 White to play.

8 White to play.

Winning by tactics

More mating attacks

These are a bit harder. White is to play and checkmate in two moves.
(Answers on page 124.)

❶ White to play.

❷ White to play.

❸ White to play.

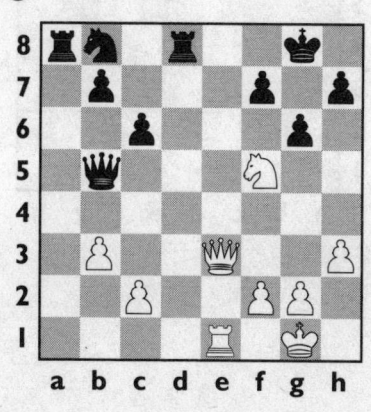

❹ White to play.

107

Winning by tactics

And finally - white checkmates in three moves.

1 White to play.

2 White to play.

3 White to play.

4 White to play.

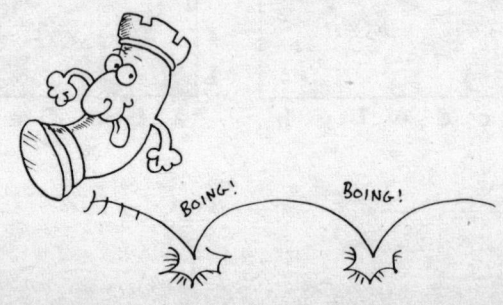

108

Winning by tactics

We have come nearly to the end of this book, and like all endings, it is the start of a new beginning. If you have read this book carefully you will soon find that you are streets ahead of your friends and can go on to further challenges.

So to help you on your future journeys, I have included some information about chess clubs and tournaments that you might like to take part in, and other books and magazines too.

See you at the world championships!

The chess scene

Some useful addresses:

British Chess Federation
9a Grand Parade
St Leonards-on-Sea
East Sussex TN38 0DD
tel: 01424 442500
email: office@bcf.org.uk

Australian Chess Federation
Mr Gary Bekker
5-10 Carawford Road
Brighton-el-fands
New South Wales
2216
tel: 61 2 9556 3960
email: gbekker@mira.net

Irish Chess Union
Mr M Cinneide
45 Harty Place
Dublin 8
tel: 353 1 7062482
email: ocinneide@ucd.ie

New Zealand Chess Federation
PO Box 216
Shortland Street
Auckland
email: nzchessfed@xtra.co.nz

Chess South Africa
Mr Arthur Kobese
PO Box 90673
Bertsham
2013 Johannesburg
tel: 27 11 985 4538

The chess scene

Join the club

Start on the road to the top by taking part in school chess tournaments. If your school hasn't got a club ask your teachers to set one up. Alternatively, get a little pocket set and challenge your friends to a game. You'll soon gather a club of chess nuts around you!

The UK Chess Challenge

One thousand schools and 35,000 players aged 6-18 take part in this, and any school or chess club can join in. Details from Mike Basman, 7 Billockby Close, Chessington, Surrey, KT9 2ED. Tel: 0181 397 1826

Local chess clubs

Most counties and major cities have junior clubs, teams and leagues. There are junior county teams at Under 9, Under 11, Under 14 and Under 18 ages, as well as separate girls teams for Under 11, Under 14 and Under 18. For details of junior chess clubs in your area, write to:
The British Chess Federation, 9a Grand Parade,
St Leonards-on-Sea, Sussex TN38 0DD.

The chess scene

The chess ladder

Start at the bottom by entering some junior events.

Standard	Grade
World Champion (Garry Kasparov)	2800
Supergrandmaster	2600
Grandmaster	2500
International Master	2400
National standard	2200
County player	2000
Club player	1600
Novice	1000
Beginner	600

The world champions

Chess has been played since at least 600AD, and probably before that. World Champions have been recognised for almost 150 years.

1886-94	Wilhelm Steinitz	Austria
1894-1921	Emanuel Lasker	Germany
1921-7	José Raoul Capablanca	Cuba
1927-35	Alexander Alekhine	Russia
1935-7	Max Euwe	The Netherlands
1937-46	Alexander Alekhine	Russia
1948-57	Mikhail Botvinnik	USSR
1957-8	Vasily Smyslov	USSR
1958-60	Mikhail Botvinnik	USSR
1960-1	Mikhail Tal	USSR
1961-3	Mikhail Botvinnik	USSR
1963-9	Tigran Petrosian	USSR
1969-72	Boris Spassky	USSR
1972-5	Bobby Fischer	USA
1975-85	Anatoly Karpov	USSR
1985-	Garry Kasparov	Russia

The chess scene

Chess books

Here is a short list of great titles to help you prepare for your World title challenge.

Subject	Title
Capturing	*Beginner to winner in two months*
Checkmating	*Find the mate!*
	Checkmate in two moves
Openings	*Secrets of chess*
	Chess traps
	How to play the opening like a master
	Silent encounter
	Chess openings
Tactics	*Two birds with one stone*
	100 death-defying chess positions
	Tactics
Endgame	*Endgames*

All available from Audio Chess, 7 Billockby Close, Chessington, Surrey KT9 2ED.

Cyber chess

Computers are tremendous to train with, because they don't let you get away with anything! (Garry Kasparov reckons that his grade improved 100 points from training with computers.) You can get good cheap computers from your local store or Dixons. National distributors are:

Chess & Bridge, 369 Euston Road, London, NW1 3AR
Tel: 020 7388 2404

Countrywide Computers Victoria House, 1 High Street, Wilburton, Cambridge CB6 3RB. Tel: 01353 740323

You can find out about chess software on the Internet site: http://www.internetchess.com/

The chess scene

Chess on the Net

General link site:
http://www.internetchess.com/

To play and get advice:
http://www.chess.net/

Deep Blue vs. Kasparov site:
http://www.chess.ibm.com/deepblue/home/html/b.html

Garry Kasparov's site:
http://www.clubkasparov.ru

To play chess online:
http://www.chessclub.com/

Chess news – The Week in Chess:
http://www.chesscenter.com/twic/twic.html

Chess shops

For chess sets, books, chess computers and software, videos, audiotapes, scorebooks, and tournament equipment.

Chess and Bridge
369 Euston Road, London NW1 3AR
(020-7388-2404)
which also publishes *Chess* magazine.

Chess Shop
69 Masbro Road, Kensington, London W14 0LS

Chess Magazine.

, Herts. EN6 3HA

for all your chess supplies
CHESS DIRECT LTD
PO BOX 18
MEXBOROUGH S64 9AR
www.chessdirect.co.uk
Tel: +44 (0) 1709 890565

The chess scene

Chess magazines

The leading magazines are:

Chess
British Chess Magazine
(see above for addresses under chess shops).

Mind Sports Olympiad

There are hundreds of other games as well as chess, and at the Mind Sports Olympiad (held in London every August) you can play them all – and win junior gold, silver and bronze medals as well!
Contact David Levy (020-7435-9496).

Chess organisations

British Chess Federation
9a Grand Parade, St Leonards-on-sea,
East Sussex, TN38 0DD
Tel: 01424 442 500

The BCF is the governing body for chess in the UK.

Chess Federation of Canada
E1-2212 Gladwin Crescent, Ottawa
ON, K1B 5N1

Promotes and encourages the knowledge, study and play of chess in Canada.

Glossary

adjournment if a game goes on too long it can be adjourned – broken off and continued at a later date.

adjudication when a game goes on too long and the result is decided according to the position on the board.

algebraic notation the method of naming the squares on the chessboard with letters and numbers.

blindfold chess chess played without sight of the board. Usually the player sits away from the board, so he or she cannot see it, and calls out the moves using algebraic notation.

blitz chess (also rapid, lightning, five-minute chess) chess played at a very fast speed, using the chess clock as a timer.

capture when one piece takes another enemy piece. The capturing piece moves on to the square of the enemy piece, and the enemy piece is removed from the board.

castling a combined move of the king and one of the rooks. The king is moved two squares along the first rank towards the rook, which is then placed on the square crossed by the king.

check a king under attack is said to be in check.

checkmate (mate) a position in which the king is under attack and cannot escape. The game ends as a win to the side that checkmates.

chess clock a double clock which measures the time taken by each player, so the game doesn't last too long.

combination a sequence of moves in which the pieces link up together to achieve an objective. A spectacular sacrifice is usually involved.

congress a chess competition or tournament, where players compete for prizes. There are thousands every year throughout the world.

correspondence chess (or postal chess) chess played by post, with players sending moves to each other through the mail.

demonstration board a large board which usually hangs on a wall and can be used to demonstrate a game to a class of pupils, or an audience. Demonstration boards are frequently used in tournaments, when the organisers do not want spectators crowding round the real board.

development a key word in chess, it means getting your pieces off the back row and into a more central position before launching an attack. The king is also usually castled, and the rooks 'connected', to 'complete development'.

diagram a picture of a chess position with pieces on it.

Glossary

discovered attack when you move a piece out of the way of another piece, and an attack on an enemy piece is uncovered, or 'discovered'.

discovered check a check that is uncovered by a piece along a straight line after a blocking piece has moved out of the way.

double check a check given by two pieces at the same time. It always involves a discovery.

doubled pawns a poor position for pawns, it happens when they are stacked on top of each other instead of being placed side by side. They cannot defend each other, and the front one gets in the way of the back one.

draw a game that cannot be won by either side is called a draw. A draw is quite common in chess – possibly a quarter of all games are drawn.

en passant a special form of pawn capture, where a pawn that has just moved up two squares can be captured by an enemy pawn standing alongside. The capture has to be made straightaway and the capturer lands on the square the enemy pawn passed over. En passant is French for 'in passing'.

en prise This means leaving a piece where it can be taken by an enemy piece, usually for nothing. In games between strong players, this sort of mistake rarely occurs, except when players are stressed or short of time.

endgame the last part of the game, where there are a few pieces on the board. Many players consider the endgame begins when the queens have been exchanged.

exchange to swap or trade pieces.

fianchetto development of a bishop on the square b2, b7, g2 or g7. It means 'little flank', and comes from the Italian *fianco*.

file a row of squares going vertically.

fork (double attack) every piece on the chess board can fork, as every piece can attack at least two enemy pieces at the same time. Making these attacks can be deadly winning weapons, as the opponent may not be able to guard both pieces at the same time.

fool's mate the shortest game, possibly ending on the second move. 1. **g4 e6** 2. **f3 Qh4++** is one example.

gambit an opening where one player gives up a piece, usually a pawn, to gain an advantage in position.

grading the ranking of players according to their strength.

hole a weakness in a position, usually a square that cannot be defended by a pawn and which is ripe for invasion.

illegal move a move that breaks the rules of chess, for example moving a knight like a bishop, or moving a king into check.

international master a title for a chess player, recognising internationally a player of great strength.

international grandmaster a rank above the international master. One of the strongest players in the world.

Glossary

j'adoube a French word, meaning 'I adjust'. This is what you say before you touch a piece if you only want to adjust it on a square, and not move or capture it.

king-side (short side) the king-side of the board is the four files e, f, g, h which are nearest to the king.

lose on time to lose a game because you did not make enough moves before your time ran out on the clock.

losing chess or suicide chess a fun game where the winner is the one who lost all his or her pieces. If a piece can be captured, it must be, and kings can be taken as well.

middle game after the opening (getting the pieces into action), the middle game begins. The players try for definite objectives – for example, increasing central control, or attacking the enemy king or pawn weaknesses.

opening the first part of the game, where the pieces are being brought into position, before the start of the attack.

pawn chain when pawns are linked together along a diagonal. The pawn further back defends the pawn further forward, like links in a chain. A difficult position to break down.

perpetual check continuous checking which results in a draw, but not checkmate.

pin a piece that holds down an enemy piece because if it moves, the piece behind will be in danger.

pocket set a small chess set that has miniature pieces, enabling games to be played on buses, trains and in other cramped places.

promotion when a pawn gets to the end of the board, it can change into a rook, knight, bishop or queen.

queen-side (long side) the four files a, b, c, d, nearest to the queen at the start of the game.

rank a row of squares going sideways.

re-capture after losing a piece to your opponent, taking a piece of same or similar value. Re-capture keeps the two opponents at level points in a game.

sacrifice a move that gives up pieces to gain an advantage, an attack, or a forced checkmate.

simultaneous display a number of games played at the same time by one player. The master usually walks around making one move at a time on the board of each of his or her opponents.

stalemate a situation where a player is not in check, but anywhere they move will put them into check. None of the other pieces can move, and the game is a draw.

strategy the planning of the long-term objectives of the game as opposed to short-term tactics and actions.

Swiss system the most popular way of playing chess tournaments, in which the players do not play everyone in the tournament, but neither is it a knockout event. Players play a selected number of opponents, and the player with

Glossary

the best overall score is the winner.

touch piece move in competition chess, touching a piece means you have to move it, unless you said 'j'adoube' first. Touching an enemy piece means you have to capture it, and putting a piece on a square and taking your hand off it means you have to leave it there.

trap a line of play to lure your opponent into a trap by allowing him or her what appears at first sight to be a good move. A trick!

value of pieces a useful way to rank the pieces. The queen = 9 points; rook = 5 points; knight = 3 points; bishop = 3 points; pawn = 1 point. The king = the game. It helps you decide which piece to exchange, and who is winning during a game.

world champion the best player in the world.

zugzwang a German word, it means that you have to move, even though the move leads to defeat. It usually occurs in the endgame.

zwischenzug a German word meaning 'in-between move'. Instead of following an expected series of moves or captures, a player inserts an in-between move which may decisively alter the course of the game.

Answers

PAGE 33 OUT OF CHECK
1. Kf2 2. Rxd6 3. Nb1 4. Kg5

PAGE 34 HOW MANY CHECKS?
1. Nc4+ Ne4+ Bg3+ b7+ (discovered check) Qe5+ Qe6+ Qxe7+ Qg3+ Qf4+ Qh6+

2. h6+ Nf5+ Bd4+ Rg6+ Rb7+

3. Qe4+ Qe3+ Qe2+ Qg6+ Qd6+ Qa6+ Qf5+ Qh3+ Qd7+ Qd5+ Qc4+ Qb3+

4. Ne3+ Ne5+ Bd3+ Bf7+ Ra4+ Rc8+ (d3 is not allowed, as it also puts white's king into check from the rook.)

PAGES 34–5 CHECKMATING
1. Qf4++ 2. Qd8++ 3. Qa6++ 4. Nf5++

PAGE 36 TEST YOURSELF: CAPTURING TESTS
1. cxd6 gxh6 Nxc1 Nxa5 Bxa6 Bxh7 Qxc1 Kxh2 Qxe6

2. exf6 Nxa2 Nxe2 Bxc8 Rxc1 Rxg7 Kxc5 Kxc6

PAGE 38 TEST YOURSELF: CAPTURES
1. Good captures: **Nxb7 Bxb7** (wins 2 points)
   Bxd8 Kxd8 (wins 6 points)
   Swaps: **cxd6 Bxd6; Nxe5 Nxe5**
   Bad captures: **Bxb5 axb5** (loses 2 points)
   Qxe6+ fxe6 (loses 8 points) **Qxh7 Rxh7** (loses 8 points)

2. Good captures: **Nxg7** (3 points) **Bxa7 Kxa7** (2 points)
   Nxd6+ (1 point)

Answers

Swaps: **Qxa4 bxa4; Rxh8 Bxh8**
Bad captures: **Nxe5 dxe5** (loses 2 points)

PAGE 71 TEST YOURSELF: DIAGONALS

1. 1. **e3** if black plays 1. ... **fxg3** 2. **Qh5++**. If 1. ... **Nf6** (to stop checkmate), white frees his bishop with 2. **exf4**.

2. 1. ... **Qh4+**. If 2. **Ke2 Qf2++**. Or 2. **g3 Nxg3**, and if 3. **hxg3 Qxh1**.

PAGE 76 TEST YOURSELF

1. 1. ... **Qxe4**. 2. **Re1** pins the black queen.

2. 1. **Nf6** (double check) **Kd8** 2. **Re8++**.

3. 1. ... **Qxd2+** 2. **Kf1 Rc1+!** 3. **Rxc1 Qxc1+** 4. **Bd1** (The queen cannot be taken because the knight at e2 is pinned.) **Qxd1+** 5. **Be1 Qxe1++**.

PAGE 79 BELITZMANN VS RUBINSTEIN

Black won with a queen sacrifice: 1. ... **Qxh2+** 2. **Kxh2 hxg3** (double check) 3. **Kg1 Rh1++**.

PAGES 79–80 TEST YOURSELF: CASTLED KING

1. 1. **Rxf6 Qxf6** 2. **Qxh7++**

2. 1. **Qe4** threatening **Qxh7++** or **Qxa8**.

3. 1. **Bh6** threatens checkmate by **Qxg7++**. Black cannot take the bishop as the pawn is pinned. To stop checkmate black must play 1. ... **g6**, which loses 2 points after 2. **Bxf8 Bxf8**.

4. 1. **Qh5** Now white threatens **Qxh7++** and attacks **f7** three times. Black's position is lost. For example: 1. ... **h6** 2. **Nxf7 Qe8** (2. ... **Rxf7** 3. **Qxf7+** is the best chance.) 3. **Nxh6** (double check) **Kh7** 4. **Nf7+ Kg8** 5. **Qh8++**.

Answers

PAGE 86 THE QUEEN MATE

WHITE	BLACK

8. Qb7

(This is by far the best move. If you choose the more obvious **Ke6** or **Kd6**, you will soon discover that you have stalemated your opponent, and the result of the game will be a draw. Instead, white makes a fence with the queen, just as in the Lawn Mower mate. The black king cannot escape from his position at the side of the board.)

8. ...	Ke8
9. Ke6	Kf8

(Running for safety, but he's not fast enough!)

10. Qf7++

10. Qf7++

PAGE 91 NO WIN SITUATIONS

Yes, white is only a point up, but white's pawn has a clear run to the end of the board. When it gets there, it can turn into a queen. And from earlier in this chapter, you will know how to checkmate then. (A good tip: don't get left with a bishop and a knight at the end of a game – keep a pawn handy so you can turn it into a queen!)

Answers

PAGES 99–100 FORKS

1. 1. **Ne8+** followed by **Nxd6**
2. 1. **Qxd5** attacking the black knight at h5 and the rook at a8
3. 1. **Nf7+** and **Nxd6**
4. 1. **Qa4+** and **Qxa6**
5. 1. **Qc8+** and **Qxb7**
6. 1. **Rf5** threatening **Rxh5** and **Rxe5**
7. 1. ... **e4** forking queen and knight
8. 1. **Qg5** threatening both **Qxd8+** and **Qxg7++**

PAGES 101–2 PINS

1. 1. ... **f4**
2. 1. **Rd1**. If black plays 1. ... **Qxc4**, white inserts the zwischenzug (in-between move) 2. **Rxd8+ Kg7** 3. **bxc4**, and comes out a rook ahead.
3. 1. **d5** attacking the pinned knight at c6
4. 1. **d4**. Not 1. **f4** because that pawn is also pinned!
5. 1. **Rxe5+**. Black cannot reply 1. ... **fxe5** because the pawn is pinned
6. 1. ... **Qxe4** 2. **dxe4 Rxd2**
7. 1. ... **f2** and the pawn queens, as the white rook is pinned.
8. 1. **Qxg6+ Kh8** 2. **Rh1++**

PAGES 103–4 DISCOVERED CHECK

1. 1. ... **d4+** and **dxc3**
2. 1. ... **Bxe5+** and **Bxd6**
3. 1. ... **Bxh2+** 2. **Nxh2 Rxd3**
4. 1. ... **Ng3+** and **Qxc2**
5. 1. **Nc5+** and **Nxa6**
6. 1. **fxg5+** and **gxh6**
7. 1. ... **Rxh3+** 2. **Kgl Rh1++**
8. 1. **Bd5+** and **Bxb7** wins a piece

123

Answers

PAGES 105–6 MATING ATTACKS

1. 1. Qe4+
2. 1. Qc4++
3. 1. Qxb7++
4. 1. Qxd6++
5. 1. Qxd7++
6. 1. Qb6++
7. 1. Qe8++
8. 1. Qe7++

PAGES 107–8 MORE MATING ATTACKS

Mate in two moves
1. 1. Nb6+ Kd8 2. Qd6++
2. 1. c3+ Ke4 2. Re3++
3. 1. Qe8+ Rxe8 2. Rxe8++
4. 1. Qxb6+ Nb7 2. Qxb7++

Mate in three moves
1. 1. Qh5+ Kg8 2. Qf7+ Kh8 or h7 3. Qxg7++
2. 1. Rxg7+ Kh8 2. Rh7+ Kg8 3. Rh8++
3. 1. Bf8+ Bh5 2. Qxh5+ gxh5 3. Rh6++
4. 1. Rc5 Ke8 2. Rf5 Kd8 3. Rf8++

Index

A
Alekhine, Alexander 25
ambush, the 65

B
bishop move 11, 17–18, 26
Botvinnik, Mikhail 39, 50
Box Mate 87–9

C
Capablanca, José Raoul 39, 58–60, 69, 93–5
captures 7, 30, 31, 35–9, 61
castling 24–5, 30, 31, 40–5, 57, 77–80
check 22–3, 30, 31, 32–5, 44–5
checkmate 7, 22–3, 30, 31, 32, 34–5, 46, 47, 62–5, 79–80, 81–9, 90, 105–8
chess clocks 84
chess clubs 8
chess computers 67
chessboards 10, 12, 27, 28–9, 31

D
Dawn Raider 66
Deep Blue 67
diagonals 10, 11, 17, 63, 67–71
discovered attack 98–9
discovered check 74, 98–9, 103–4
double check 98

E
en passant 40, 48–50
en prise 45
Euwe, Max 47

F
fianchetto 56
files 10

Fischer, Bobby 61
forks 16, 96, 99–100

G
gambit 58, 59
Giuoco Piano 71–3
grandmasters 6, 70

I
International Masters 6, 80

J
Janowski, David 58–60

K
Karpov, Anatoly 64, 91
Kasparov, Garry 67, 75
king move 11, 21, 26
knight fork *see* forks
knight move 11, 15–16, 26

L
Lasker, Emanuel 23
Lawn Mower Mate 81–3, 87

N
notation 28–31

O
opening 55–60

P
pawn move 10, 12–14, 26, 48–50
pins 97–8, 101–2
Polgar, Judith 91

Q
Queen Mate 84–7
queen move 11, 20, 26

Index

R
ranks 10
re-captures 36–7, 38
resignation 50–1
rook move 11, 19–20, 26

S
sacrifice 58
Scholar's Mate 62–5
Spielmann, Rudolf 93–5
stalemate 40, 46–7, 90–1
Steinitz, Wilhelm 16

T
touch piece move 50

W
World Champions 16, 23, 25, 47, 50, 61, 64, 75, 91

Z
zigzag attack 65
zugzwang 53

super.activ
All you need to know

0 340 773294	Acting	£3.99	☐
0 340 764686	Athletics	£3.99	☐
0 340 791578	Basketball	£3.99	☐
0 340 791535	Cartooning	£3.99	☐
0 340 791624	Chess	£3.99	☐
0 340 791586	Computers Unlimited	£3.99	☐
0 340 79156X	Cricket	£3.99	☐
0 340 791594	Drawing	£3.99	☐
0 340 791632	Film-making	£3.99	☐
0 340 791675	Fishing	£3.99	☐
0 340 791519	Football	£3.99	☐
0 340 76466X	Golf	£3.99	☐
0 340 778970	Gymnastics	£3.99	☐
0 340 791527	In-line Skating	£3.99	☐
0 340 749504	Karate	£3.99	☐
0 340 791640	The Internet	£3.99	☐
0 340 791683	Memory Workout	£3.99	☐
0 340 736283	Pop Music	£3.99	☐
0 340 791551	Riding	£3.99	☐
0 340 791659	Rugby	£3.99	☐
0 340 791608	Skateboarding	£3.99	☐
0 340 791667	Snowboarding	£3.99	☐
0 340 791616	Swimming	£3.99	☐
0 340 764465	Tennis	£3.99	☐
0 340 773332	Writing	£3.99	☐
0 340 791543	Your Own Website	£3.99	☐

Turn the page to find out how to order these books.

ORDER FORM

Books in the super.activ series are available at your local bookshop, or can be ordered direct from the publisher. A complete list of titles is given on the previous page. Just tick the titles you would like and complete the details below. Prices and availability are subject to change without prior notice.

Please enclose a cheque or postal order made payable to Bookpoint Ltd, and send to: Hodder Children's Books, Cash Sales Dept, Bookpoint, 39 Milton Park, Abingdon, Oxon OX14 4TD. Email address: orders@bookpoint.co.uk.

If you would prefer to pay by credit card, our call centre team would be delighted to take your order by telephone. Our direct line is 01235 400414 (lines open 9.00 am – 6.00 pm, Monday to Saturday; 24-hour message answering service). Alternatively you can send a fax on 01235 400454.

Title .... First name .... Surname
....

Address ....

....

....

Daytime tel .... Postcode......................................

If you would prefer to post a credit card order, please complete the following.

Please debit my Visa/Access/Diner's Card/American Express

(delete as applicable) card number:

Signature ....Expiry Date ....

If you would NOT like to receive further